Stop obsessing about everything that could go wrong *Make an accurate assessment of the real risks* *Cope with feelings of anxiety and stress* *Begin to again

DBQ633774

COPING

WITH

UNCERTAINTY

10 simple solutions

BRUCE EIMER, PH.D. & MOSHE S. TOREM, M.D.

Foreword by Sylvester Johnson, Police Commissioner, Philadelphia Police Dept.

This timely book provides a beacon of light in a world full of shadows and provides us with assistance for the anxieties we all face.

> —George Litman, M.D., Medical Director, Heart Center, Akron General Medical Center, Akron, Ohio

The authors have clearly recognized the reality of human frailty and responded to our quest for wholeness in our lives by offering an imaginative and manageable series of coping mechanisms.

> —Rabbi Robert S. Leib, Old York Road Temple-Beth Am, Abington, PA

Many of us live in constant fear that something bad is bound to happen. This book gives sound suggestions which can help us break the habit of worrying.

> —Rev. Verlin Barnett, Director of Spiritual Care Department, Akron General Medical Center, Akron, Ohio

COPING
WITH
UNCERTAINTY

10 simple solutions

BRUCE EIMER, PH.D. & MOSHE S. TOREM, M.D.
Foreword by Sylvester Johnson

New Harbinger Publications, Inc.

Publisher's Note

This publication is designed to provide accurate and authoritative information in regard to the subject matter covered. It is sold with the understanding that the publisher is not engaged in rendering psychological, financial, legal, or other professional services. If expert assistance or counseling is needed, the services of a competent professional should be sought.

Distributed in the U.S.A. by Publishers Group West; in Canada by Raincoast Books; in Great Britain by Airlift Book Company, Ltd.; in South Africa by Real Books, Ltd.; in Australia by Boobook; and in New Zealand by Tandem Press.

Cover design by Amy Shoup
Edited by Kayla Sussell
Book design by Michele Waters

ISBN 1-57224-296-5 Paperback

Printed in the United States of America

New Harbinger Publications' Web site address: www.newharbinger.com

04   03   02

10   9   8   7   6   5   4   3   2   1

First printing

I dedicate this book to my wife, Andrea, whose love and companionship help me to cope with uncertainty.

—Bruce N. Eimer

I dedicate this book to my wife, Ronit Adrienne, whose love and encouragement have enabled me to write this book.

—Moshe S. Torem

Contents

Foreword vii

Preface xi

Acknowledgments xiii

Introduction 1

1 Accept Uncertainty as Part of Life 7

2 Evaluate Your Real Risks 19

3 Change Obsessive Thoughts 27

4 Restore Inner Harmony   43

5 Release Tension   53

6 Improve Your Tolerance for   65
    Frustration

7 Develop Healthy Self-Acceptance   83

8 Learn to Forgive   97

9 Connect with Others and Create   111
    Meaning

10 Learn to Be Flexible   123

    Summary   133

    References   135

Foreword

Modern life is filled with uncertainty and insecurity. A large part of police work and law enforcement involves resolving uncertainty and improving security. That, in turn, involves the use of psychology. Since September 11th, 2001, public safety has become a much more daunting challenge than it used to be. Naturally, people are searching for ways to help them feel safer and more secure. Psychology offers some helpful answers.

This book was written by a clinical psychologist and a psychiatrist. Working as a team they have arrived at some helpful ideas about how we can maintain a reasonable level of personal comfort in the midst of uncertainties. Doctors Eimer and Torem, two experienced clinicians and stress management professionals, offer ten simple solutions for mastering uncertainty and making it less fearful. After reading their solutions, I feel that I now have new tools for handling challenging uncertainties.

During my many years in law enforcement, I have encountered numerous challenging situations, filled with tension and lots of uncertainty, in which split-second decisions were required that determined life or death. In many of those situations, and afterwards, I experienced a great deal of stress; a normal reaction to extreme situations and challenges. Unless such intense stress is acknowledged and managed appropriately, it can accumulate to unhealthy proportions. Thus, I've learned the importance of processing stress reactions in a healthy manner. This is doable, and a matter of survival.

Doctors Eimer and Torem are experts at teaching the nuts and bolts of how to manage stress. In their book, they address both stress that is preventable and stress that isn't. It is essential that members of police departments, law enforcement agencies, fire departments, emergency medical crews, and other security agencies become skilled and well-rehearsed in their management of their occupational and personal stress. This book is an excellent new source of valuable information for the different schools that train new recruits.

I believe it is vitally important to incorporate the coping skills that Doctors Eimer and Torem present here in the formal training of new recruits. This book is a real treasure trove, not only of information, but also of practical skills and exercises that anyone can learn and practice in their day-to-day life. It is written in a down-to-earth, accessible style that citizens from all walks of life will find easy to understand; moreover, it is fun to read. It presents truly practical usable information, not academic jargon.

This little book is comprised of ten chapters. Each chapter provides a simple but eloquent practical solution for dealing with aspects of uncertainty in daily life. I found the perspective that the doctors offer on how to control one's own thought processes especially helpful. The connection they draw between one's thoughts and the way one feels emotionally and physically is also very helpful. Many of the exercises here can really help you to change unhelpful beliefs and habits.

In police work, where every action matters, it is of paramount importance to be able to let go of and release tension and stress so that they do not build up to unhealthy levels. In this book, the doctors teach you how to do this. Furthermore, Doctors Eimer and Torem teach you how to improve your tolerance for frustration, which will empower anyone who deals with frustration regularly, on-the-job, or in daily life. The authors offer practical advice on how to defuse the buildup of unhealthy emotional feelings, and by so doing, reduce stress, and the vulnerability to illness.

By practicing the techniques described by Doctors Eimer and Torem, and careful reading of the case examples, anyone in any stressful walk of life (most walks of life!) will become better equipped to function more effectively and maintain a happier state of mind. So, read on, and learn to be your own effective stress manager.

—Sylvester Johnson
Philadelphia Police Commissioner
Philadelphia, Pennsylvania

Preface

If you want to give God a good laugh, tell him your plans.

—Old Yiddish folk saying

Who knows what the world will be like twenty years from now, let alone in five years? The only thing we know for sure is that *change* and *uncertainty* will continue, and that those who know how to adjust to change and uncertainty will live more comfortably and successfully. Unfortunately, the life skills you need for coping with change and uncertainty are not taught in school.

So, we aimed at making this book as timeless and as positive as we could. In this way we hoped to make it relevant for the moment, and pertinent for the years to come. Uncertainty is an ever-present issue, as is the need to cope with it. This has always been so and probably always will be so.

For many people, it is often the cumulative stress of the small hassles of daily life that gets to them, or contributes to their eventual ill health by precipitating stress-related disorders.

This book focuses on how to build coping skills for anything that life may serve up. So, with that as our goal, we wrote this book. We hope that it makes a positive difference.

—Bruce N. Eimer
Moshe S. Torem

Acknowledgments

First of all, we acknowledge and thank our families for standing by us and giving us the strength and encouragement to complete this project. We thank and acknowledge our editors at New Harbinger, Dr. Matthew McKay and Catharine Sutker, for recognizing the importance of this book and supporting its publication. We also thank Kayla Sussell for her dedicated, thoughtful, and creative help and support in the editing process, Michele Waters for easing our book into its final form, and Amy Shoup for designing our book's attractive cover.

Introduction

Nothing's ever for sure. That's the only thing I'm sure of.

—Akiva Goldsman,
A Beautiful Mind

This book is designed to address the problem of having to live with uncertainty at different times in your life. Uncertainty is a condition in which you lack knowledge or confidence about what will happen to you in your daily life as it relates to your job, financial security, health, wellness, shelter, family, and safety on a personal, family, and community level.

The way you deal with uncertainty has an impact on your overall health and well-being. Successful coping with uncertainty is necessary and essential to leading a productive and happy life. Unsuccessful coping with uncertainty has unhealthy effects on your mind and your body.

The key point to coping successfully with uncertainty is to stay calm, keep a cool head, and apply logical, rational, and effective ways to mastering the perils of uncertainty. Staying calm means controlling the intensity of your negative emotions, such as anxiety, fear, anger, grief, sadness, rage, helplessness, alienation, cynicism, and the feeling that you have no future.

When these emotions are not controlled, they impede your ability to think clearly and to process the information and facts around you in an effective and organized fashion. Staying calm is a way of taming your emotional brain so that your executive, logical brain can rationally assess the facts in the present and plan your actions to be the most effective for your day-to-day living.

The payoff for staying calm in the face of uncertainty is that you are able to see your options and choices more clearly and thus make the right choices. Staying calm enables you to ignore matters that could intrude and hinder you from achieving your goals. Here, we are referring to distractions that create noise and more anxiety.

The costs of not staying calm in the face of uncertainty involve damaging your health, family life, effectiveness on the job, and the possibility of ending up feeling miserable and hopeless. When uncertainty is not effectively managed, your body may become a dumping ground, and you may experience a variety of bothersome physical symptoms.

Ineffective management of chronic uncertainty can lead to a chronic sense of feeling alienated from society. This can manifest in the form of cynicism, rejection of all moral and religious principles, and the feeling that life has no meaning, causing you to feel lost, dejected, and adrift, without purpose or direction.

The Purpose of This Book

We start from the point of view that uncertainty is a fact of life. We believe that all uncertainty is fruitful, as long as it is accompanied by the wish to understand. On the other hand, uncertainty becomes an unnecessary burden when the fact of its reality is accompanied by the wish to deny that it exists, avoid the unknown, and by maladaptive efforts to manufacture evidence for certainty.

The purpose of this book is to present you with ten simple solutions that you can learn and then use to cope effectively with the fact of uncertainty in daily life. When you learn to use these solutions, and practice them in your day-to-day living, you will lead a happier existence.

Nowadays, there seem to be more reasons to be afraid than in previous decades. The world is a more uncertain place than ever. There has been a sharp increase in the frequency of terrorist acts around the world, including in the United States. People are living with the threat of further terrorism, and the television and news media provide a continual stream of information that heightens the focus on these threats. Understandably, all of this has led many people to feel frightened of what the future may bring.

Since the 1990s, many people, with good reason, have become less trusting in general, given increased media exposure of new kinds of scams, and a wide range of ways in which innocent people have been criminally victimized. Threats of violence, domestic and international, wars around the world, unstable and oppressive governments, and the use of terror also have contributed to instability. This has been reflected in a major change in the stability of the world economy. In addition, technology is changing at a pace that can be described conservatively as "warp speed." All of this change, instability, and uncertainty has made people feel more vulnerable.

Vulnerability stems from the feeling that one has no control over the outcomes of what happens in the world. Feeling vulnerable leads people to feel more endangered and threatened. It can shatter our basic sense of trust and security in the world, our belief that the world is a safe place to live in, and our expectations that we will be here tomorrow. Our vulnerability can become a breeding ground for fears of all types, and erode our feelings of comfort and security in carrying on our day-to-day activities. The lack of adequate support and connectedness to other people can also become a breeding ground for alienation.

Given all the instability and uncertainty in our world today, our purpose in writing this brief book is to empower you by giving you ten simple and practical solutions for coping with uncertainty. These solutions can help you to counter your feelings of vulnerability, fear, and alienation, and aid you in mastering your fears of the future. We hope that this book will be of use in coping with the uncharted waters of the twenty-first century.

The book is organized into ten chapters. Each chapter presents a key problem or specific problems associated with dysfunctional coping with uncertainty. You are then shown new ways of viewing the problem, out of which emerge a coping solution or a class of coping solutions for the problem. We then give you clear and simple exercises for realizing the essence of the coping solution.

Each chapter guides you through a sequential process of developing coping skills for mastering your anxieties and fears of the future, and managing uncertainty in the present. Beginning with chapter 1, you are helped to accept that uncertainty is a part of life. In chapter 2, a solution is discussed for evaluating your real risks in different uncertain situations. We use rational, cognitive-behavioral strategies to accomplish this, and help you distinguish between the *probability* of a feared event occurring or reoccurring and the *possibility* that it can. We then help you to face your fears armed with this new knowledge and confidence.

Chapter 3 shows you how to change obsessive thoughts, and chapter 4 teaches you ways to restore healthy harmony between your mind and body. Chapter 5 describes ways to release physical and mental tensions and reduce nervousness. Chapter 6 presents techniques to improve your tolerance for frustration. Chapter 7 focuses on ways to develop healthy self-acceptance, which is a cornerstone for healthy coping, as well as for preventing and alleviating depression.

Chapter 8 addresses the related problems of anger, guilt, and depression by teaching you how to forgive yourself and others. Chapter 9 discusses building healthy connections with others and creating meaning in your life. We also discuss the advantages of finding your purpose in life. Everyone has a purpose in living, although not everyone may be aware of their purpose. Finally, in chapter 10, we address ways to develop greater flexibility so that you can better cope with change. This is the tenth step or solution.

Dr. Rollo May, the famous psychologist once said that anxiety is essential to the human condition. He believed that the confrontation with anxiety can relieve us from boredom, sharpen our sensitivity, and assure the presence of just enough tension necessary to help us survive and thrive. We wholeheartedly agree.

Accept Uncertainty as Part of Life

The quest for certainty blocks the search for meaning. Uncertainty is the very condition to impel man to unfold his powers.

—Erich Fromm

Accept uncertainty as a part of life because it is. Your moods and feeling states are affected and determined not only by the events that you encounter, but also by how you view those events and what you believe. This idea is not new; it is based on traditions of wisdom dating back many millennia. Therefore, an important step in coping with uncertainty is to learn how to identify your thoughts, and understand how they activate your feelings and physical sensations in response to stress.

The famous ancient Greek philosopher, Epictetus, recognized long ago that *as we think, so shall we feel* when he made the following famous statement, *"Men are disturbed not by things but by the views which they take of them."* The Buddha, too, is reputed to have said, *"All that we are is the results of our thoughts."*

Two of the guiding principles in this book are (1) whenever you feel *bad*, there is an underlying stress-producing thought, and (2) your thoughts, feelings, physical sensations, and behaviors are all connected. Therefore, we will teach you a number of ways to accomplish the following:

1. To use your stressful feelings as a cue to look for stress-producing thoughts.

2. To identify which thoughts create distress, and which create comfort.

3. To challenge and refute (or dispute) your stress-producing thoughts.

4. To reframe and change them.

Yogi Berra, the famous catcher and then manager for the New York Yankees, when asked about the changes he chose to make in his life, once quipped, "When you reach a fork in the road, take it." What he no doubt meant was that we have no choice but to choose choice when life presents us with choices. Life repeatedly presents us with challenges and opportunities. In fact, the Chinese symbol for crisis or adversity can also be read as *opportunity*. Following this logic, *luck* is the successful meeting of *opportunity* and *preparedness*.

Some of you may hold the belief that *certainty is a birthright and that uncertainty should not exist*. What you no doubt mean by this belief and feeling is that you *should* or *must* know the exact outcomes of your actions and behaviors in daily life. However, the truth is that *uncertainty* should be a part of your conscious life because it is. No one can predict with 100 percent certainty the exact outcomes of our actions in daily living. No one can predict the future with certainty. The future is being created continually in the present. Today is the first day of the rest of your life, and tomorrow's past.

How many of us would want to know the exact date of our eventual death? We don't think many. That's because, what if it were next week, or next year? Fortunately, in this world, it is not possible to know such a thing. That is because even the thought that it *could be* possible to ever know such a thing is based on the assumption that the date is somehow predetermined. We hold that to be a false assumption. The future is not predetermined.

We have all heard the saying, "I have a date with *destiny.*" By this, do people believe destiny to mean that their *fate* is fixed? Some might interpret this saying in this manner. However, we believe that it is more adaptive and functional to view *destiny* and *fate* as being continually under construction. You continually create your own future in the present by your ongoing attitudes, beliefs, choices, and actions. Let's take a mundane example.

When you get up in the morning to wash up and brush your teeth, you expect to have clean running water in your bathroom. However, it is possible that one day you may face the simple reality of dirty brown water coming out of your faucet, or having no water at all. How you view this problem becomes the key to effectively coping with it. Do you view this hassle as a sign that your enemies have deliberately acted to poison you or make your life difficult? Do you view this problem as God punishing you for your sins? Do you see the situation as a result of your stupidity or personal negligence in maintaining the plumbing in good working condition? Or, do you see the problem as a simple fact of chance in life that could happen to anyone?

How you view this simple event will determine what you do about it, and how much of a hassle it proves to be.

A New Way to Think About the Problem

It is extremely important to realize that many frustrating events in your daily life are the result of pure chance and have nothing to do with any intentionality of a Higher Power, your neighbors, or other people. This point of view will help you to accept the simple fact that uncertainty and the unexpected are a natural part of normal day-to-day living. The acceptance of this idea is a key to crafting effective solutions when faced with unforeseen events.

A Practical Solution

The key to solving unexpected problems is to accept the fact that uncertainty is a part of life, to stay calm, and to accept that there is a problem that must be solved. This will enable you to analyze the facts of the problematic situation, so that you can fashion a practical solution and focus on remedying the problem.

It is extremely important to stay focused; that is, to avoid getting distracted or sidetracked by other issues coming from the past, issues related to conflicts you may have with other people, or issues coming from other people's agendas unrelated to your problem at hand.

For example, faced with the unexpected problem of no clean water coming out of your faucets in the morning, keeping a cool head can allow you to focus on assessing the problem and what needs to be done about it. One helpful way to handle the situation might be to call some of your neighbors and see whether they too have this problem. The information you get will help you to isolate the cause of the problem, and plan your next step. If the problem is isolated to your own home, you might focus on checking the running water in all the faucets in your house, or the valve on the main water line to see if it is on or off. If you cannot determine the source of the problem, you may find it necessary to call a plumber. On the other hand, if your neighbors have the problem too, then a different approach may be necessary, such as calling the local water department or municipal authority.

Exercising the Solution

This first exercise provides you with an opportunity to practice handling one type of common everyday uncertainty that most of us encounter fairly often. By practicing this solution exercise, you will develop the healthy habit of creative problem-solving in the face of uncertainty.

Imagine you have a scheduled appointment with your dentist or doctor. You know from previous experience that it takes between ten to fifteen minutes to get to the doctor's office. You leave your home fifteen minutes ahead of time. As you are driving on your usual route, you encounter a traffic slowdown which eventually crawls to a total standstill. You have now encountered a fact of life—uncertainty. A trip that you had expected to take no more than ten to fifteen minutes may now take much longer, but you have no idea how long you will be delayed. So, what are you going to do?

As you sit in your car, you have several choices. One choice is to get angry and honk the horn, bang the steering wheel, yell out the window, or just fume inside yourself. Obviously these are dysfunctional responses because they do not bring you to an effective solution for the problem at hand. Instead, you might practice the following:

First, gather more information about the cause of the traffic standstill by opening the window and signaling the drivers coming from the opposite direction to inform you of the cause of the traffic slowdown. This information will help you to assess the best solution, which in this case may be calling your doctor's office to inform them about the reason for your delay. In addition, you may look for the option of getting off of your regular route on to a side street that will lead to the doctor's office using a different route.

This rational response is practical and clearly focused on the problem at hand. It helps you avoid personalizing the problem with such maladaptive and dysfunctional responses as self-blame and unnecessary anger at the cars in front of you. It helps keep you from getting angry at other drivers or at yourself. Successfully practicing this solution exercise will enhance your sense of mastery and self-confidence, thereby empowering you to continue with creative problem-solving in the future. It is important to keep in mind, however, that doing the above is easier said than done.

The famous Danish philosopher Soren Kierkegaard (2000) was correct when he stated that "anxiety is the dizziness of freedom." The solution we have just described is *simple* but not necessarily *easy*. If you are like most people, it is a reflex to become frustrated and then angry when your direct route to achieving your goal is blocked or thwarted. However, remember that just because something comes naturally to you, it isn't necessarily good for you to do it, or inevitable. Frustration need not lead to hostility or aggression.

There are choice points (opportunities to choose among different response options) *before* anger is triggered, and once it is triggered, as to how it is handled and expressed. Frustration is healthy. It can serve as a motivator in the search for an effective alternative solution to the problem at hand. However, while it may be normal to feel angry in certain situations, it is not always or even usually healthy. Anger can cloud your brain and serve as a distracter from finding a solution to the problem. Although it may temporarily block the anxiety or pain, anger seldom helps in finding a viable solution.

Now, what can you do if you are driving on a crowded freeway or highway and traffic comes to a standstill? You hear on the radio that a bad accident eight miles ahead has halted all traffic. What do you do?

The best solution would be to take a few deep breaths and accept that you are going to be delayed. If you have a cellular phone with you, you can call the doctor's office, or wherever you have your appointment, and explain why you will be late. At this point, you *are* stuck in traffic. You cannot get out of the traffic jam. But you do have choices regarding how you handle this frustration (this is a "choice point"). Do you lose your cool and start screaming and having a tantrum? Do you let that little voice inside your head keep reminding you about how much of an inconvenience this unexpected delay is going to be? Or, do you keep a cool head and accept that the best choice is to "go with the flow"? Going with the flow would mean relaxing, perhaps putting a good CD or tape on and listening to it. You can prepare beforehand by keeping a few tapes or CDs handy so that you have the right one for your mood.

So, if you practice the above exercise faithfully, you may allow yourself to get frustrated up to a point. However, when you catch yourself beginning to blame yourself, the other drivers on the road, fate, a Higher Power, and so on, you need to tell yourself something like, "Stop! Anger will get me nowhere. This is an opportunity (choice point) for me to practice patience and creative problem-solving. I can do this!"

John's Story

John is a thirty-seven-year-old, self-employed accountant. He is very organized, self-disciplined, and extremely responsible. He is proud of his accomplishments on the job and at home. He believes that a responsible man should be prepared for anything that occurs at home or on the job. He also believes that every negative event has a reason originating from human error or incompetence.

One morning, John was awakened by a phone call from the superintendent of the building in which his office is located informing him that there had been a break-in at his office and many of his files were disorganized and scattered all over the floor. John experienced an immediate feeling of anxiety and panic. When he drove to his office, many thoughts came to his mind. He was wondering who could have done this and whether he knew the person. Then, he obsessed on the thought that he might have forgotten to lock the door when he left the office the previous night. This thought made him feel incompetent and angry with himself. "How could I have done that?" he thought. "Am I losing my mind? Am I losing my grip? I can't stand not knowing how such a thing could happen! I must have done something to cause this. . . . There must be a reason. I have to find out."

As John entered the office, he felt a sinking sensation in the pit of his stomach and a lump in his throat. His hands were perspiring, and he felt as if his heart was going to jump out of his chest. When he saw the mess, he became enraged, and had the urge to throw the files at the wall or out of the window. After that thought, he proceeded to fantasize finding the perpetrator and beating him up.

Feeling a sense of helplessness and fearful of losing control, he called his wife to inform her of what had happened. John's wife, Sarah, is a very calm, compassionate, and loving person. She listened to John and sensed his high level of distress as he vacillated between self-blame and the rage he felt toward the person who had done this. She came over to the office immediately and helped John to realize that the first thing to do was to call the police. The police's preliminary investigation determined that the door had been locked at the time of the break-in. They also knew that there had been a series of similar office burglaries in the area.

Sarah listened empathetically to John's distress and helped him to recognize that the break-in had not been personally directed against him, and that he had done nothing to cause it. This helped John to realize that uncertainty is part of everyone's life. This realization helped John to stop his self-blaming and quieted his rage, allowing him to focus instead on a practical series of solutions with the goal of getting his office back in working order. In addition, John decided to investigate installing a burglar alarm system.

John felt much better after expressing his feelings and concerns to his wife. He felt that he had been listened to and understood by her without being criticized or blamed. She also helped him realize that sometimes events happen that we have no control over, and that the most important thing is to keep a cool head focused on the practical solution to the problem at hand.

When you accept that uncertainty is a part of life, you are less likely to personalize it and rage about it. As the old adage puts it, *the only certainties in life are death and taxes*. Everything else is uncertain. Life is about making meaning from uncertainty; making inferences, and drawing conclusions from incomplete information. When you change the way you think about uncertainty and reeducate yourself about its necessity and inevitability, you can refocus your attention on coping. This helps to make your life meaningful.

The word *should* means *ought to be* or *must be*. However, if something does not exist, it is counter to reality to insist that it *should*. Certainty does not exist in the world. There is no way to know what the future will bring with certainty. Conversely, if something does exist, it is counter to reality to insist that it *should not*. Uncertainty does exist in the world. We can lead more fulfilling lives by learning to co-exist with it and cope with it. This increases our sense of control.

A Practical Solution to "Shoulding"

The famous psychologist and psychotherapist Dr. Albert Ellis is fond of saying "Stop *shoulding* on yourself" (Ellis 1998). He asserts that demanding certainty about anything and whining when you don't get it, is one of the main causes of human neurosis. This point of view was also expressed by Karen Horney, a psychiatrist and psychoanalyst, who coined the term, the "tyranny of the shoulds" (Horney 1993). Accepting that uncertainty is part of life enables you to overcome the "tyranny of the shoulds." This process is easier if you follow these *four* simple steps adapted from Schwartz (1996).

Exercising the Solution

1. *Relabel* the word "should." Instead, use the words *can*, *want*, *desire*, or *wish*. You can want something, but that does not necessarily mean you'll get it, or *have to* have it.

2. *Reframe* your view of the consequences of not getting what you want. It may be inconvenient, but in all likelihood, you'll survive. Learning to accept and handle *not* getting what you want will make you stronger and more resilient.

3. *Reeducate* yourself about your available options and alternatives (choice points). If you cannot have certainty about something (really about anything), you can still create a good chance of getting what you want, or something else that is acceptable, and avoiding what you don't want. Remember, you have choices.

4. *Refocus* your attention and energies on setting realistic goals and working hard to achieve them, but don't let this curtail your imagination. It has been said that, *what the mind can conceive, the mind and body can achieve*. However, you have to be willing to work hard to achieve what you want. It is important to stay focused on *your* actions. By doing so, you keep yourself centered and you stay functional.

An important lesson can be learned from cases of "miraculous recoveries" from usually fatal diseases, such as certain types of cancer and aggressive infectious diseases such as anthrax.

Recently, several survivors of usually fatal inhalation anthrax reported that they didn't know how they survived (acceptance of uncertainty), but they asserted that they never gave up hope. They explained in post-recovery interviews that they kept up their strong faith in the goodness and benevolence of God or a Higher Power, were able to accept whatever happened in the end, and maintained a basic feeling of trust in their own strength and their body's natural wisdom. They also reported having a lot of love, a good support system, and a focus on health (Johnson 2001). This combination of factors also is evident in other cases of so-called "miraculous recoveries" from cancer.

Cancer specialists Doctors Carl and Stephanie Simonton emphasized imaging health and a successful battle against cancer cells as part of their cancer treatment protocol. What people often fail to consider when invoking the Simontons' work on the "cancer fighting attitude" (Simonton, Simonton, Matthews, and Creighton 1991) is that there are other essential elements: acceptance of uncertainty, faith in a Higher Power, acceptance of reality and of what is, trust, love, fortitude, a good support system, good medical care, and a positive focus on health.

In sum, it is adaptive and healthy to accept that which you cannot change. You cannot change the fact that uncertainty is a part of life. When you accept that you cannot predict the future with certainty, you gain strength because you shift your focus to the present. In reality, the present is all there is. By making choices in the present, you gain a stronger hand in creating your own future.

We end this chapter with Reinhold Niebuhr's famous Serenity Prayer:

> God, grant me the serenity to accept the things I cannot change, the courage to change the things I can, and the wisdom to know the difference.

Evaluate Your Real Risks

To be alive at all involves some risk.

> —Harold MacMillan, former prime
> minister of Great Britain

Evaluate your real risks so you can prepare yourself to deal with any eventuality. You can do much better at controlling your anxiety about the uncertain future, especially in situations that you fear, by accurately evaluating the real risks involved. When you feel afraid, you tend to believe that your worst fears are just around the corner. Most of the time this is not so. Most of the time, "fight or flight" is unnecessary. However, in those rare circumstances when your worst fears are just around the corner, your odds of survival increase greatly when you are prepared with knowledge, the necessary coping skills, and a clear, cool head.

When you worry, you overestimate the threat or risks associated with uncertainty, and you underestimate your resources for handling it. The bigger you perceive the threat to be and the smaller you perceive your resources to be, the more anxiety you tend to have. Anxiety is a signal that there may be danger ahead. It is associated with apprehension, dread, nervousness, fear, and avoidance. Anxiety is adaptive when it notifies us of real or potential harm and, then, keeps us out of harm's way. However, it is maladaptive when it acts like a false alarm, triggering fear and apprehension when there is no objective danger to be wary of, or threat to fear.

When fear escalates out of control, it can paralyze you and cause you to avoid everything associated with the object of your fear. It then can lead to inaction or rash actions that are usually maladaptive and self-defeating. For these reasons, at his first inaugural address, President Franklin Delano Roosevelt told the world that *"The only thing we have to fear is fear itself."*

Donna's Story

Donna is a forty-two-year-old school teacher who won a round trip vacation to Hawaii as a result of having been selected Teacher of the Year in a large city school district. When she learned the news, however, she did not rejoice but became panicky. A friend noticed that she seemed unhappy, and asked her what was the matter. Donna confided that she very much wanted to go to Hawaii on her vacation but she was afraid of flying. In her mind, flying was associated with planes blowing up in the air and crashing on take-off and landing. Donna also felt trapped and out of control whenever she thought about getting on a plane. Her memories of flying were associated with sitting as stiff as a board, glued to her chair, holding on to the armrests with white knuckles, being short of breath, and having a very rapid heartbeat.

Because she wanted so much to go, she decided to seek therapy for her problem. At the initial interview, it was determined that Donna had once had a white-knuckle flying experience with some really bad turbulence. That was the last time that she had flown.

At that session, Donna also learned that her belief that flying was dangerous was based on her overestimating the risks associated with flying on a commercial airplane and her false assumption that driving was much safer. This assumption allowed her to drive daily with little fear of having a serious car accident, but it prevented her from getting on an airplane. Because the reality is clearly in favor of flying as much safer than driving, her misinformation prevented her from seeing the issue realistically, and it unnecessarily limited her travel options.

A New Way to Think About the Problem

Persistent worrying and avoidance in the face of uncertainty are associated with confusing the concepts of *possibility* and *probability*. Possibility refers to the fact that a certain event *can* in fact take place, regardless of how slim the chances really are. Probability, on the other hand, refers to the likelihood that a certain event *may* occur beyond the pure chance.

An event that is very unlikely to occur, such as being hit on the head by a falling meteor, is a possibility (that means it can happen), however, the probability of it occurring is extremely unlikely. Therefore, people walk outdoors without wearing steel helmets to protect themselves from falling meteors.

Treating a possibility as a probability is, in fact, a distortion of reality, and a manifestation of overestimating the real risk of a possible dreaded event occurring. This confusion between possibility and probability was partly responsible for Donna's flying phobia.

As her sessions continued, Donna learned that the reason she had developed her fear of flying was related to her confusion about the concepts of *possibility* and *probability*. She learned to recognize that even though there is a *possibility* that the plane she would be traveling on could crash, the *probability* of this happening was very low. In fact, Donna continued to drive every day in spite of the reality that there was a much greater probability of getting into a fatal car accident than dying in a plane crash. She was helped to reach the conclusion that flying is not risky and is, in fact, much safer than driving a car. She came to this new belief after gathering factual information about the comparative risks of flying versus driving.

A Practical Solution

The essence of the solution to this problem of overestimating the threat or risk associated with uncertainty is to clarify the difference between possibility and probability. This makes it possible for you to accurately evaluate the real risks.

When you realize that something dreadful, something that you have been worrying about, is certainly possible but the chance or probability of it occurring in actuality is extremely remote, you will automatically feel better. Then, you can shift your focus of attention to something else. Let's continue with Donna's story:

Eventually, Donna learned to change the way she thought about flying. She acknowledged the truth of the fact that flying actually is much safer than many other activities in addition to driving, such as riding a bicycle, skiing, swimming in the ocean, crossing a busy street in the downtown section of a large city, and so on. This led her to realize that it was in her best interest to master her fear of flying once and for all. So, she took the important step of booking the trip to Hawaii and actually making the trip.

In preparation for her trip, Donna was instructed in the use of guided imagery. This enabled her to imagine having a successful experience flying. Then, she was helped to internalize the experience, so that she would feel confident about flying. This was done by helping Donna to play different images and thoughts in her mind. Then, Donna practiced mental imagery on her own, which helped her to become more prepared psychologically for her trip. As expected, her trip went very smoothly and was actually pleasurable since she had changed her images and thoughts. Her mastery of this flying experience empowered her to continue to use air transportation comfortably when the necessity arose.

It is most adaptive to face your fears armed with knowledge. Many of the events you are afraid of, and consequently avoid, are possible but extremely improbable. That means that the odds (or probability) of their happening are extremely low. Knowing that these are the facts of a particular fear can give you the confidence to face that fear and do what you have been afraid of doing.

Many of us drive our cars on busy roads and expressways crossing bridges that stretch over deep ravines or bodies of water. Every now and then you may have a thought cross your mind like, "What if there's an earthquake and the bridge collapses? My car and I will plunge into the water." You may even experience physical and emotional symptoms associated with such a thought. However, most of us continue to drive on expressways and over bridges because we know that even though there is a possibility that a bridge may collapse, the probability of that actually happening remains extremely low. We take the chance of driving over bridges, and by doing so, we master our fears and empower ourselves.

Exercising the Solution

The next time you know that you are going to drive on an expressway or over a bridge, prepare yourself before you get into your car by using a simple mental exercise. Assess the probability versus the possibility of the expressway or bridge collapsing. How do you do that? First, consider your odds of surviving your trip across that stretch of highway. Ask yourself the following questions:

- How many people cross it every day, every week, every month, and every year?

The answer is *many.*

- How many times have you crossed it or a similar structure, and how many times has the bridge collapsed?

Your most likely answer is *never.*

- How frequently do highway bridges collapse?

The answer is that *it is extremely rare for highway bridges to collapse unless there is a truly powerful earthquake.*

- What are the odds of a powerful earthquake occurring just at the moment that you are in the middle of that bridge?

The answer is that *the odds are extremely small*!

In conclusion, your most likely risk assessment will be that the risk of the bridge collapsing is tiny. After you do this simple mental exercise, and come to this conclusion on your own, you will feel more comfortable. You will notice that comfort while you are driving over the bridge and afterwards as well. So, just take your trip and empower yourself.

In truth, we are often more frightened than circumstances warrant. Our troubles spring more often from what we imagine and fantasize than from external reality. In today's fast-paced information age, we are continually barraged with information and live, up-to-the-minute, breaking news. The news is comprised of events that make a "story." "News" means what is new. Events that are commonplace do not fit the bill for "news." So, the news media jump on potential "stories," and sometimes even makes them up when "real stories" are sparse.

Thousands of airplanes take off and land every day. However, you are unlikely to see a news report with the headline, "Two Thousand Planes Took Off and Landed Safely Every Day This Week Without Even One Uncomfortable Incident." Yet, if you did, it is more likely that you would develop the expectation that flying is very safe; in fact, safer than driving.

There is another issue having to do with numbers and probabilities that is important to mention here. That is, there are quite a few carjackings these days. Does this mean that there is a greater probability of getting car-jacked? Not necessarily. Part of the reason for the greater number of carjackings may be that there are more cars on the road today than ever. When horse and buggies, stagecoaches, and the railroad were the main means of transportation, there weren't any carjackings, but there were quite a few stagecoach holdups, and armed train robberies.

Consider another fact. There are many more carjackings every year than there are plane hijackings. Now, when a car is carjacked, it may make the local news, but it seldom makes the national or international news. However, if a plane is hijacked, it makes the national and international news, as it should. But does this mean that the risk of a plane that you're on being hijacked is greater than the risk of you being car-jacked? Certainly not. Furthermore, your risk of being car-jacked is very small, especially if you take appropriate precautions (locking doors, staying alert, not driving through bad neighborhoods, etc.).

Another issue to consider is that when you are driving, you are in control. You are at the wheel and you feel your control. In contrast, when you are a passenger on a commercial airliner, you are not in control of the plane; the pilots are. But, when you are on a plane, it is important to keep in mind that the plane is your instrument of transportation and the pilots are your agents whose job is to operate that instrument and get you to your destination safely with the greatest ease and convenience. The pilots are well trained to serve as your agents, and because they are on that plane with you, they also serve as their own agents, which gives them all the more reason to operate that plane safely. This realization and way of thinking will allow you to relinquish your control comfortably. You might even enjoy not having to be in control for a while!

In conclusion, you can minimize your tendency to worry by keeping in mind the difference between possibility and probability whenever you feel apprehension about a dreaded event occurring. Recognize that our fears spring more often from what we imagine and fantasize than from external reality. Understand that an event can be reported as taking place more often than it used to happen, yet the probability of it happening to you still may be very small. Finally, learn to relinquish gracefully your need to be in control over events that are not in your control.

When you think in these ways, you will more accurately evaluate the real risks associated with feared events and other situations. You will be less likely to overestimate the risks. As a result, you will feel more confident, less fearful, and you will empower yourself.

Change Obsessive Thoughts

As a rule, what is out of sight disturbs men's minds more seriously than what they see.

—Julius Caesar

Change obsessive thoughts so you don't waste energy worrying. It is quite common to deal with uncertainty about the future by thinking repetitive thoughts and worrying about what possibly could happen to you. Sometimes these thoughts can take on a life of their own. It is your mind's way of trying to control the underlying anxiety and fear you have of uncertainty. However, sometimes this solution can become the problem when these repetitive thoughts and worries turn into obsessions.

Having obsessions is like paying interest on trouble before it falls due! This is because they not only fail to control the underlying anxiety adequately, they also make us more uncomfortable because we experience them as intrusive and alien to our sense of self. Our failure to stop and control these thoughts feeds uncomfortable feelings of helplessness, incompetence, and vulnerability. As the old Swedish proverb states, "Worry gives a small thing a big shadow."

A New Way to Think About the Problem

It is very important to view obsessions not as your enemies but rather as your brain's unsuccessful attempts to control your underlying fear and anxiety about the unknown. Viewing obsessions in this new way allows you to change the way you think about this problem. Instead of fighting the obsessions by telling yourself to "stop obsessing" or "stop thinking this way, this is crazy," you can begin to reeducate your brain to control the underlying anxiety in a new and more functional way. This redefinition of the problem is the key to the solution.

A Practical Solution

The essence of the solution to the problem of repeatedly obsessing about disasters is to change your obsessive thoughts.

As you repeatedly practice this solution, it will become a habit. You will experience satisfaction as you notice ongoing changes in the nature of your thoughts and how you respond to your thoughts. This process involves the following four steps:

1. The first step is described above. It requires *redefining* the problem.

2. The second step entails *reeducating* your brain to believe that repeatedly thinking about the worst possible disaster is dysfunctional, ineffective, and does not solve the problem. In fact, it becomes a problem of its own. Reeducating yourself helps you to recognize that this circular, repetitive way of thinking must be changed into a more functional and effective way of managing your anxiety.

3. The third step involves *refocusing* your thoughts. Refocusing entails an active shift into thinking, feeling, and
doing something different. One of the most successful
ways to refocus your thoughts is to change what you
are doing at the moment you become aware you are
obsessing. For example, imagine driving and becoming
aware of your obsessive thoughts about possible disasters on the road ahead. One effective way to refocus
would be to turn on the radio to your favorite station
and listen to country music, classical, jazz, or pop. Or
you could have an already prepared tape with your
favorite mood music. You could listen to the music
and, as you do that, sing along or hum to the music.
This solution shifts your brain's present awareness into
a new focus; one associated with a feeling of pleasure
as well as different images and thoughts. This is one
way to change the channel your thoughts are tuned to;
or to change the station broadcasting in your brain.

4. The fourth step involves *reframing* your view of the
problem; that is, changing the way you think about it.
This is best accomplished when you are in a calm state
and can think about the problem and possible solutions without getting hot under the collar.

Exercising the Solution

Here are a number of exercises that you can practice to change
your obsessive thinking or behavior.

1. When you find yourself obsessing about disasters, and
you are at home watching the television news, you can
change the channel to another one. You can also turn
off the TV and turn on your radio or CD player and
listen to your favorite music.

You can also shift your focus in this way if you find yourself obsessing during whatever activity you are doing (e.g., sewing, reading, washing dishes, and so on). Just turn your attention wholly onto the activity. Be mindful of what you are doing; how it feels, etc. Stay in the present. Or, you might focus on some interesting aspect of what you are doing; for example, stop reading and think about the content of the reading material for a while, or concentrate on the texture of the fabric you are sewing, the feel of the soap suds, and so on.

To make this solution more powerful and effective, to give it a "zing," you can literally *exercise* the solution. You could start doing aerobic dancing to your favorite "get up and go" music. This activity exercises your body, improves the circulation to your muscles and brain, and shifts your attention to a totally new state of awareness. Shifting your attention is a very effective way to stop dysfunctional obsessions.

2. Humor can be very useful. It literally can help you to "lighten up." Watching or listening to funny people can activate laughter and joy. Consider adding videotapes and/or audiotapes of your favorite stand-up comedians or movie comics to your collection, for those times when you need to tune-up your body, mind, and spirit.

Interestingly, the employment of humor, especially "gallows humor," is one way that people who work together in intensive situations laced with uncertainty cope with their collective and individual anxieties and fears. Understandably, the "right" to use such humor around members of the group is reserved solely for those who are considered peers, and who have been through similar experiences. For example, years ago, when one of us worked in residential treatment facilities for severely emotionally disturbed and developmentally disabled children, we often had little warning before we had to defuse and deal with a child's physical blowup. Since we worked together as peers in emotionally and physically demanding situations, we depended on one another; and because we cared about the children, we felt we had earned the license, *among ourselves,* to occasionally use humor when unwinding at the end of a day. This helped reenergize us for another trying day.

Here is another exercise that you can practice anywhere, whenever you realize you are obsessing on unwanted thoughts.

3. From now on, the moment you realize that you are obsessing, interrupt your negative obsessions by yelling the word *Stop!* in your mind. Imagine hearing an authoritative, calming, and reassuring voice in your head (perhaps the voice of someone you greatly respect or are in awe of), ordering your brain to *Stop Obsessing Right Now!*

You can even visualize an appropriate image of an authority figure to reinforce this verbal order, such as a kind police officer or teacher standing in front of you with his or her hand raised. Or, you could choose to visualize a big red stop sign, a military or police blockade or barrier, perhaps even a big dog barking at you to stop!

Whatever image you choose will work for you because it is *your* choice. This is an easy exercise and it will enable you to stop the obsessing. However, stay safe. *Never do the visualization part of this or any other exercise while operating machinery or driving.*

Note: Interrupting the activity you were doing when you caught yourself obsessing, will interrupt or break the mind-body state in which you were trapped in an endless loop of obsessive, repetitive, unwanted thoughts.

4. A fourth way to interrupt obsessing is to pick something interesting to look at, to concentrate on, and to focus your visual attention. While looking at this object, take three or four very slow deep breaths. Slowly breathe in relaxation and slowly exhale tension and stress with each slow deep breath. Never do this while driving or operating machinery.

5. A fifth way to change repetitive, obsessive thinking is to recognize that you have other choices and options that apply to solving the problem at hand (choice points). Pushing harder and harder against an immovable stone wall will not get the wall to move. However, backing off and rethinking possible solutions to the problem will likely produce better results.

All too often, we do more of the same even though it is not effective, hoping that increasing our efforts will work. But it does not. Consider the following scene in your imagination:

You are walking down a beautiful country road in the woods. This road leads to a beautiful lake and you want to go there and relax for a while. Suddenly, you encounter a high stone wall cutting right across your path and blocking your way. This barrier extends far into the woods on both sides of the path. You are completely blocked from proceeding. Somehow you need to get over, around, or through this solid stone wall. First, you try to climb it, but you cannot. Next, you try pushing against it, but it doesn't budge. Your frustration grows and your attempts become frantic.

The voice in your head says: "You are blocked. There is nothing you can do but turn back." However, you do not follow this advice. You are so determined to get past this wall, you bloody your hands from trying so hard. How can you get to the other side of the wall? More of the same is certainly not the answer. So, where does the solution lie? A change in the way you think about the problem will lead to a change in what you do about it.

You can calmly look to the right and left of the path, near the wall, for a small trail or a footpath you could follow that might lead somewhere—to take you to a door, a gate, or to the end of the wall.

*Doesn't this make more sense than bloodying your
hands? So, that's what you do, and eventually you
discover a small clearing and a trail on your left
near the wall. You follow it and are joyfully relieved
to find an unlocked gate that goes through the wall
to the other side. There, you come upon a
flower-covered meadow leading to that serene lake
on the other side.*

The solution to your problem was not to push harder and
harder, continuing the same actions that hadn't worked in the
first place. The solution was to recognize that you had several
choices of what to do open to you (choice points), and to make
a different choice. Solving the problem was just a matter of
changing your thinking and behavior.

6. The case example below describes a sixth method for
   interrupting obsessions and then changing the obsessive state. Read the case example and feel free to modify the content of the imagery to suit your individual
   needs. *Because you can do the following exercise by
   choosing your own imagery, the method described in
   Tina's story will work for you, too.*

Tina's Story

Tina is a twenty-six-year-old married police officer with
two children. In her work she is frequently the first
emergency-aid person to appear on the scene of serious car
accidents, fires, and medical emergencies. This repeated exposure to critical traumas in her everyday work has instilled a
sense of fear in her, along with anxiety-producing obsessive
worries involving "what if" scenarios should such disasters
befall her or her loved ones.

One day, Tina talked to a peer counselor, who suggested
to Tina that instead of trying to analyze away her obsessive
worries, it might be more functional for her to *shift the focus*

of her attention to something else. In this way, Tina would be able to *interrupt* her obsessions. Of course, Tina asked the counselor, "What if I cannot keep my mind off of my worrisome thoughts?"

The counselor answered that Tina would be pleasantly surprised to discover that she could deal with these "what if" concerns easily and simply. The counselor instructed Tina to do the following exercise. As you read through this exercise, feel free to modify the imagery to suit your individual needs.

When you find yourself caught up in an unending loop of repetitive, upsetting thoughts, what you are doing is obsessing. What you can do instead is the following: Take a minute or two to situate yourself in a safe place where you will be undisturbed. Make sure you are not operating any machinery or driving when you do this exercise.

> *Close your eyes and take a deep deep breath. Slowly exhale, let your eyes relax, and let your body float. Open a new channel of concentration whereby you experience yourself dancing with a handsome young man (woman) on a very romantic date. The DJ is playing your favorite music. Notice the rhythm and the smoothness with which you and your date are swinging together in harmony with the music. Pay attention to the look in his (her) eyes and see them as two shining stars looking at you with joy and kindness. See him (her) smiling at you with his (her) beautiful smile. Experience the warmth of his (her) hand touching your hand. Take a deep breath through your nose and experience the pleasurable scent of his (her) aftershave lotion (perfume). Now take in all of these pleasurable sensations and enjoy them.*
>
> *When you open your eyes and you can focus again, you become fully alert and awake, and allow a relaxing smile to spread across your face that imprints your new, relaxed state of mind, as well as*

your surprised satisfaction about how well this has worked for you.

Any of the exercises described above can work for you. They all enable you to interrupt obsessive thinking and change the channel on your repetitive thoughts. Each exercise provides a key to open "brain lock" (Schwartz 1996). The essence of each solution choice involves *redefining* the problem, *reeducating* your brain, *refocusing* your attention and your thinking, and *reframing* your view of the problem; that is, changing the way you think about it.

Scheduling "Worry Time"

By now, hopefully, you have experienced the powers of your imagination and the healing effects of relaxation. You have a better understanding of uncertainty and how, up until now, you have been coping with it. You also have a better understanding of worry, how you do it, and what it is related to.

However, before we move on, there is one more exercise that is of significant value. It involves *scheduling worry time.* The basic idea is that worrying is actually a way to avoid dealing with your underlying fears. When worrying, you actually go round and round thinking the same thoughts over and over again. This enables you to avoid facing the real problem, which is your underlying anxiety that you will not be able to handle the dreaded event or experience. You may feel helpless to change this because, often, our worries seem to take on a life of their own.

Scheduling worry time puts you back in charge. It also helps you to face the real problem causing your anxiety. What you do is allow yourself to worry—and do nothing else but worry—at a designated time, for a fixed amount of time (either fifteen or twenty minutes exactly), at a designated place (usually in your home where you will not be disturbed), a specified

number of times each day (usually two sessions a day are suffi-
cient). After your "worry session" is over (it is best to set a
timer), you stop worrying and go back to your business. Any-
time during the day that you catch yourself worrying, you
remind yourself that you must stop and save it for your next
worry session.

It's as simple as that. Start scheduling worry time and see
how well it works. Give it a week and if you remain disci-
plined, you will find that you are worrying less and less, and
staying calm and relaxed more and more. You will also find
that your worries seem to dissipate. What you were worried
about becomes less important.

When the Past Intrudes into the Present

Sometimes, past hurts have a way of being reactivated by present hurts or challenges. When this is the case, it is important to
recognize that the past exists *only* in memories. This realization
will give you a way to liberate yourself from past hurts that
keep intruding into the present. The means for doing this
involves reviewing the negative meanings that you continue to
assign to hurts or traumas you suffered in the past. This is best
done by following these steps:

1. The first step is to find a safe place where you can be
   by yourself or with a trusted person.

2. Second, use a technique to relax away your physical
   and mental tensions and stress. Different relaxation,
   focusing, and quieting exercises are described throughout this book. Some involve paying attention to your
   breathing. Others involve progressively relaxing the
   different parts of your body. Still others involve the
   healthy use of your imagination.

3. Third, from your place of safety in the present, employ your imagination and your memory to review the past experience that is haunting you. Our memories are not perfect. Don't expect to recall the past event accurately. The goal is not to uncover or discover any sort of truth about what happened. Rather, the goal is to face your current ideas about the past hurt that are still bothering you. Remember this motto: *That which we resist tends to persist*. It is healthy to face whatever has been bothering you, rather than continue to suppress it. Keep in mind, however, that we are not suggesting doing this repeatedly for an indefinite length of time. The goal is to do it adequately a few times, so the past can be laid to rest, and you can go on living your present life to create a new future that is more to your liking.

4. The fourth step is to identify the main stress-producing thoughts that you continue to replay in your mind about the hurtful situation.

5. After you have identified these thoughts (choose one or two main ones), it is time to rethink and revise these thoughts; these negative conclusions you have about *yourself* that until now you have accepted; and have connected to your hurtful, past experience. This is done by coming up with evidence that does not support and, in fact, refutes your negative conclusions. You can do this by asking yourself:

- What does this situation mean about me?

- How do I know this is true?

- Is there a possible distortion in my thinking? What might it be?

- Is there another way to look at it?

- What would I tell a good friend who went through the same thing?

- What new thoughts would make me feel better?
- Can I now mentally rehearse a better outcome?

6. The sixth step requires you to use your imagination to envision a healthier, more comfortable future that raises your self-regard and self-confidence. You may benefit from writing it down and then reading it to yourself several times. Be specific about the change that you would like to see and experience in your future, and what you would like to remain unchanged. Try to cover as much detail as possible in your written description.

If the past issue you are dealing with has a life of its own, or does not feel safe to deal with on your own, then this type of work is best done with the help of a professional therapist. You will know if this is so. It is your responsibility to take care of yourself. If this is the case, do not do this exercise on your own. There are many other exercises in this book that you can do that will help you to feel better and cope better with uncertainty.

Zarren's Scrolling Blackboard Technique

We all have the ability to revise our perceptions and our memories. There is nothing mysterious about any of this. We do it every day in small ways. The following is a script you can use called "Zarren's Scrolling Blackboard Technique" (Eimer 2002; Zarren and Eimer 2001) that will direct you in doing this in an effective way.

You can do the following exercise either with your eyes closed or with your eyes open. Either way is fine. If you choose to do it with your eyes closed, first read the script several times so you know how to do the exercise. If you choose to do the exercise with your eyes open, just read along slowly, and experience what comes up for you. We are going to guide you to do some exploration of the past. Following this script will enable you to begin to erase problems from the past that are no longer relevant, and leave them behind where they can do you no harm.

Do you remember when you were in school and each classroom had a blackboard on which you could write with chalk and erase what you wrote when you wanted to? Imagine such a place now, with a blackboard that you can write on in your imagination. Imagine that this is a modern blackboard with an automatic scrolling feature that allows you to write a lot, and it will scroll to produce more space, as you need it, like a word processor. Make sure that you imagine a modern blackboard with this scrolling feature.

Now take a piece of chalk off the blackboard ledge and go back as far as you can in your mind, and start writing everything you can remember that was hurtful, harmful, fearful, uncomfortable, or emotionally unpleasant. Include your physical hurts as well as your emotional ones. Be as detailed as you can be. Include people, places, and things.

Don't be concerned about how long it takes you to accomplish this task. When you use your imagination, time is very flexible. What you imagine feels like a long time could be only a short time in reality, and what feels like a short time could really cover a long period of your life. Be as thorough as you can, and take as much time as you need.

Notice that as you finish writing with your chalk on a section of the blackboard, it automatically scrolls up, and a clean panel is available for more of your writing. Make sure that your blackboard is working well mechanically.

Write everything that you possibly can, right up to the present time. Then, look at the blackboard and note that it is scrolling back to the beginning! This allows you to check everything that you have written to make sure that you haven't left anything out. If you need to add anything, extra space will appear for you. Check everything that you wrote. Good.

Now, take the eraser off the shelf, and starting with the bottom-most recent item that you have written, begin to erase it. Notice that the blackboard scroll function is working in reverse. Erase every bit of writing that you see. Wipe the slate clean. Remove all of the events that you wrote about which caused you to hurt, whether they were physical or emotional. Wipe them out. Remove them. Leave no trace. Take whatever time you need and erase every bit of it. Don't leave anything.

When you have wiped the slate clean, go back and remove any remnants that may be left. When you have completed this, simply relax. Just continue to sit for a while, feeling how relaxed you are and how very comfortable you are. When your deepest mind (your unconscious) gets the idea that it can maintain the comfort you have obtained from this exercise, and also continue to process, in a nonintrusive way, any remaining remnants, blink your eyes, open them wide, and come back fully alert, sound in mind, sound in body, and in control of your feelings.

How do you feel now compared to before you began this exercise? You can benefit by using this "scrolling blackboard" technique over the next several weeks to "wipe your emotional slate clean." In fact, you may wish to add this procedure to your daily routines. This addition will not require much time. By doing so, you will be freeing up psychological energy to cope more effectively in the present and stay calm in the face of new uncertainties as they arise. It will enable you to process and deal with any "leftover remnants" that come to mind. Your level of anxiety will be significantly reduced by doing this because the buildup of hurt that has, until now, been responsible for some of your emotional discomfort will be dissipated.

After you do this for a week, reevaluate how you feel. Notice that you feel lighter, more energetic, and stronger, as if you are carrying less baggage, less "emotional baggage," with you. If there is a cumulative buildup of emotional stress that needs to be erased, you can take out your "scrolling black-board" whenever you need it. By doing this, you will ease your burdens, and find it easier to stay calm in the face of new uncertainties and challenges.

The value of this exercise is enhanced by a wise observation the philosopher Soren Kierkegaard (2000) made:

> "Life can be understood backwards but it must be lived forward."

Restore Inner Harmony

The sound body is the product of the sound mind.

—George Bernard Shaw

Restore inner harmony so your mind and body function together as one. Some people experience fear and worry in times of uncertainty in the form of one or more of these uncomfortable physical sensations: muscle tension; headaches; back pain; indigestion; palpitations; blurred vision; dizziness; shortness of breath; excessive sweating; insomnia; fatigue; irritable bowels; frequent urination; irregular menstrual cycles; nausea; dry mouth; hoarseness; a lump in the throat; and so forth. When this happens, the person may not have any conscious awareness that any of these symptoms may be, in fact, a manifestation of underlying anxiety and worry. The individual's body has become a "dumping ground" for the person's fears, anxieties, worries, and resentments.

When people become consciously aware of their physical symptoms, that awareness can turn into what they choose to focus on, and such a focus will distract their minds from the original source of their anxiety. The new fears and worries about their physical symptoms may become one more layer on the surface of their minds, about which they have conscious awareness.

Many people who suffer from persistent stress-related physical symptoms become worried about having an underlying physical disease. Usually, they seek out medical specialists and request examinations and laboratory tests to find the physical disease that they believe will explain their physical symptoms. Most of the time their searches are fruitless, and the reassurance they receive is short-lived. This is usually followed by even more anxiety and worry.

In these situations, it may be more useful to *redefine* the problem, so that a new definition can lead to a more effective solution. There is no reason to allow anxiety about uncertainty to turn our bodies into dumping grounds!

A New Way to Think About the Problem

After medical disease has been ruled out as the cause of your physical discomfort, it is of the utmost importance for you to consider that your physical sensations may be caused by your underlying anxieties and worries. Careful consideration of this concept will lead you directly to the solution; that is, to the idea of learning how to manage and control your underlying anxieties and tensions.

The strong connection between the mind and the body has been proven in scientific research, and it is reflected in our language, as well. English is rich in expressions that demonstrate how the mind and body affect each other in numerous intricate ways. Here are a few common examples:

- He is so disgusting, he makes me sick to my stomach.

- My inability to put an end to the problem was eating me up inside.

- He is such an irritating pest, he gets under my skin.

- This job is giving me a headache.

- He was so controlling that, in his presence, I was choking for air from the rage I felt.

- He is so annoying, a real pain in the neck.

Some Practical Solutions

All of the solutions for dealing with these kinds of feelings are aimed at restoring a healthy harmony between your mind and your body. The essence of the solutions described below is to create experiences that provide healing mind-body tune-ups. Consider the following solution options:

The Language and Labels You Use. The *first solution* option (choice point) is to become more conscious of the language you use in your self-talk, and change the words you use to talk to yourself. Remember, we all talk to ourselves. We all have inner voices that comment on what is happening around us, motivate us, and direct our behavior. This is normal as long as we understand that these inner voices are manifestations of our own thoughts, and they are a part of us.

When you catch yourself describing your feelings to yourself in language that is self-defeating, self-destructive, or that reinforces your discomfort, you can simply change the language you use to *words of comfort*. For example, your job doesn't have to "give you a headache," it can just be "frustrating." Your inability to solve a problem immediately need not "eat you up inside," it can be "the motivation to seek other solutions." When someone irritates you, she doesn't have to "get under your skin," her behavior can simply be labeled as "annoying" or "irritating." These three examples illustrate the importance and feasibility of using language *consciously.* *You can now practice becoming aware of your negative mind-body self-talk and start changing it.* Be aware of how you talk to yourself. Be kind to yourself.

Affirmations. *Affirmations* are positive statements to repeat to yourself that validate, affirm, and reinforce your strengths and your well-being. Some other terms for affirmations are *ego boosters* or *ego strengtheners.* Writing, memorizing, and mentally repeating meaningful affirmations for yourself is a *second solution option.* Our minds create our reality of the past, the present, and the future. Thus, training your mind to visualize your goals, and repeating a positive affirmation several times a day are two powerful methods for shaping a new reality in your mind. When you repeatedly practive new ideas and behaviors, they are fixed in place, or *imprinted* in your unconscious mind. Repetition imprints a new reality.

That reality can then be manifested in actuality through discipline and determination. Walt Disney once said, "If you can dream it, you can do it." We now know that if you can imagine it, you can improve your chances to achieve it.

An Affirmation Exercise

Now for the *second solution,* let's create your own specific, individualized affirmation. The exercise is to write several lines that have affirmative meaning for you. If you have not already done so, get a blank notebook to serve as your personal journal to regularly write in your affirmations.

For example, Elizabeth, a twenty-seven-year-old manager of a fast-food restaurant, was suffering from intense worry and uncertainty focused on her job, the unpredictability and insufficiency of her income, and the instability of her marriage. So, she tried applying the principles of repetitive positive thinking to counter all of the worrying she was doing. She visualized desirable goals in her daily life regarding her health, marriage, and the goals she hoped to accomplish at work. As a therapeutic exercise, she wrote in her journal several times a day. Here are some of the individualized affirmations she created for herself:

> *I, Elizabeth, am a human being. As all human beings are, I am entitled to have my feelings. I have the full range of human feelings. I cope well with these feelings. I move forward with my goals in my personal life, at home, and at work. I apply well my knowledge, my experience, and my wisdom. Every day in every way I am getting better and better. My mind is clear, my thoughts are more focused. My feelings are more positive. My body and mind, spirit and soul work well together, in harmony, creativity, and wisdom.*

Now, pick up your journal and write your own special affirmation. One that speaks to your desires and validates your physical, emotional, and spiritual needs. Take your time doing this, and, remember, it's your own special affirmation—so tailor it to *your* life and *your* needs. As your life changes, you can change your affirmation as you see fit—it's yours; it will work well for you.

Mini-Vacations. A *third solution* is to take "mini-vacations" throughout the day. Take breaks and imagine yourself in your favorite, relaxing, safe place. Think about what you especially like about that place, and, as you remember why you like it, feel the happy feelings. By doing this, you can break up the mental and physical tensions that accumulate during your workday, and restore harmony between your mind and body.

Breaks. When you take short stretching or exercise breaks during the day, you release accumulated physical tension, so you feel more comfortable and think more clearly. When you take a few minutes to do short mental exercises, for example, saying your affirmations or writing them in your journal, you release mental tension and stop the buildup of stress in your body. Using these methods, the negative energies do not accumulate and turn your body into a dumping ground. So these negative energies do not manifest in your body in the form of headaches and other physical symptoms.

Clearing Energy Blockages

A *fourth solution* to the problem of accumulated mental tension and physical discomfort is to clear out stagnant energy blockages in your body to get your energy to flow more freely. The following exercise will allow you to do that by exercising your senses in a neutral, healing, and pleasant way.

1. Begin by sitting in a comfortable, supportive chair with your back upright and your feet flat on the floor. Separate your hands and let them rest palms down on your lap. Take a deep, deep breath. Hold it for a few seconds. As you slowly exhale, close your eyes, let your eyes relax, and allow your body to float.

2. Continue to breathe comfortably in and out at your own natural pace. Be aware of the air flowing in and filling your lungs with an abundance of oxygen; then, as you exhale and let the air flow out, notice the ease and effortlessness with which this happens. With each exhalation, permit yourself to breathe out all of your tensions, all of your worries, all of your anxieties, and all of your stress. Allow these negative energies to flow out and leave your body.

3. Now, open a new channel of concentration whereby you begin to slowly mentally scan your entire body from the top of your head to the bottoms of your feet. When you come across an area that feels tense or blocked, stop scanning and focus all of your attention

on that area. Imagine your breath flowing through that area washing it clean of any impurities, blockages, or waste products.

4. If you can reach the area with your hands, place one hand palm down on the spot and direct healing energy, however you imagine it, from your palm and fingertips into that area with each exhalation. Also, imagine pulling negative energy out of that area like a magnet into your palm and fingertips with each inhalation. If you cannot reach the spot, just imagine the energy flowing between your hand and the spot. It works just as well. After doing this for a little while, shake the negative energy out of your hand into the air. After clearing an area, continue your body scan and move on to any other areas that need clearing. When you find another such area, repeat the process just described.

5. After you have scanned your entire body, permit yourself to exercise each of your additional senses. First listen to the sounds in the room around you. Then, open a new channel of concentration whereby you imagine (or listen to in actuality) some really pleasant healing sounds or relaxing music. Focus on this for a little while as it clears your auditory channels of concentration and makes you more receptive to healing sounds. Then, move on to your next sense.

6. Next, take a deep breath through your nose and experience your surroundings with your sense of smell. Then, open a new channel of concentration whereby you experience some really pleasant healing scents and aromas. Focus on this for a little while to clear your olfactory channels. Then, move on to your next sense.

7. Next, open your eyes and focus your visual attention on something interesting in the room not too far away. Study the object. Then, close your eyes and hold

onto the visual image. Continue to look at the object with your eyes closed. Whatever you continue to see is just fine. You are exercising your visual memory and clearing your visual channels. Focus on this for a little while. Then, move on to your next sense.

8. You have already exercised and cleared your tactile (touch), kinesthetic (physical sensations), auditory (hearing), olfactory (smell), and visual senses. Now, move on to your last sense, your sense of taste. Imagine biting into your favorite fruit or other healthy, organic whole food. Or, imagine sipping your favorite beverage (e.g., coffee, tea, juice). Savor the taste and feel your salivary glands being activated. Focus on these taste impressions for a little while and enjoy them.

9. After exercising all of your senses in these ways, allow your mind to wander. When you are ready to shift gears again, take a deep, deep breath, and as you exhale, allow any last remnants of tension, stress, discomfort, or negative energy to flow out of your body.

10. When you are ready, gently open your eyelids and allow your eyes to come back to focus. See the objects around you become clear in all of their natural beauty. Allow a pleasant smile to spread across your face for having taken the time to experience this healing mind-body tune-up. You are now ready to return to your activities of the day, or to continue reading this text, with more energy, vitality, serenity, and calm focus.

Practice this exercise on a regular basis. At the beginning of your practice, do it several times a day. Later, you become so skilled at it, and at activating the relaxation response, that each exercise may take you just five to seven minutes. The long-lasting effects of this exercise are invaluable for achieving mental serenity, focus on the present moment, mindfulness, physical relaxation, and for developing mind-body harmony and tranquility.

Randy's Story

Randy told her doctor that she felt angry all the time but she didn't know why. She was under his care for acid reflux, which was causing frequent symptoms of heartburn, indigestion, stomach cramps, diarrhea, a tight chest, and a lump in her throat. Her doctor suspected stress was contributing to her symptoms, so he asked her to do several things in addition to taking the medicine he prescribed.

First, he asked her to keep a journal to record the times when her symptoms worsened, to note what was going on at the time, and what her thoughts, feelings, and behaviors were. He also asked her to record what she had been doing, thinking, and feeling earlier in the day and the night before. Writing in her journal helped Randy to discover that her angry, resentful thoughts were the most powerful triggers for her symptoms. Randy's doctor also asked her to do the following *focusing* exercise when she was symptomatic:

Sit down in a comfortable chair with your feet flat on the floor, close your eyes, and breathe normally. Place your hands on the area of discomfort (stomach and chest) and observe your physical sensations. What do they remind you of? What do they feel like? Notice what thoughts, images, and feelings come up.

Ask your stomach, chest, and throat what they are trying to tell you. Are you neglecting something important? Wasting your energy on something unimportant? Stressing your body unnecessarily? Eating foods that you shouldn't? Eating feelings you need not swallow? Holding on to feelings that you can let go of? Taking blame for something that's not your responsibility? Blaming too much? Wallowing in resentment, hate, or other destructive emotions?

Staying fired up too long when you're frustrated? Let your mind act as a receiver and notice what thoughts and feelings come up for you.

When you are ready, take a deep breath, count from one to five, and at five, open your eyes and return to focus feeling wide awake, alert, and comfortable. Write in your notebook journal any insights you have obtained.

By doing the focusing exercise and writing in her journal, Randy learned that the lump in her throat was connected to "swallowing" her rage and resentments, the stomach cramps and tight chest were connected to feeling victimized, helpless, and fearful, and her diarrhea was connected to feeling afraid, driven, and overwhelmed. This knowledge helped Randy to gain greater mastery over her symptoms and to attain improved inner harmony.

Follow the principles we have gone over, and practice any of these exercises, and your anxieties and worries will no longer turn your body into a toxic dumping ground. Your fears, anxieties, worries, and resentments will no longer be stored in your physical body. You now have choices as to how you can process and dispose of the physical manifestations of your negative emotions.

Release 5 Tension

*Sometimes the most important thing in a whole
day is the rest we take between two deep breaths.*

—Etty Hilesum

Release tension so you can renew and replenish yourself. At
times, you face situations in which you experience stress that
has no outlet. This means that your body may experience some
sort of tension without any clear or specific physical symptom.
When people who experience this are asked what it is they feel
or experience, they frequently say, "I am upset but I don't
know why," or "I am distressed and I have no idea why."

Many people who experience this condition tend to act
out their sense of distress by engaging in unhealthy behaviors
and habits like alcohol and drug abuse, overeating, smoking,
gambling, sexual promiscuity, impulsive spending, and other
impulsive behaviors. Often the attempts to cure them of their

dysfunctional and self-destructive behaviors are unsuccessful when using educational or insight-oriented methods alone.

A New Way to Think About the Problem

It is helpful to redefine this problem as distressed feelings and pent-up tensions seeking an outlet. Acting-out and impulsive behaviors function as a release outlet for these tensions. However, in and of themselves, these behaviors often become heavy-duty secondary issues due to their addictive and self-destructive characteristics. The essence of understanding these types of problems in a new way involves redesigning the existing maladaptive expressive outlet to becoming a more flexible and protective release outlet, one that can serve your own true best interests.

Practical Solutions

The essence of the solution to this problem has two aspects. The first is relaxing away tension. In chapter 4, we covered several ways to do this. The second aspect is to find safe and appropriate outlets for expressing, ventilating, and releasing your stress and pent-up feelings.

Relaxing Away Tension. When you are relaxed, you cannot be angry or upset, anxious or afraid, frustrated or stressed, because relaxation is the physical and emotional opposite of all of those uncomfortable feelings. So, it is adaptive to learn what it feels like to be comfortably relaxed. Then you can build up a memory of comfortable relaxation that you can rely on to relax yourself whenever you need to. In this chapter, and in those that follow, we shall continue teaching you different ways to relax wherever you are and whenever you need to do so, easily and comfortably.

Finding Outlets for Releasing Stress

Practical solutions for releasing stress involve the implementation of activities designed to accomplish one of two goals: (1) to discharge physical and mental tension, or (2) to transform maladaptive, self-destructive behaviors into adaptive, self-protective behaviors. There are many safe activities that can serve as a way to discharge tension. These include physical pursuits such as aerobic exercising, target shooting at a range, gardening, sewing, working around the house, and so on.

The transformation of maladaptive, self-destructive behaviors into adaptive, self-protective behaviors can be brought about through activities that produce increased awareness about the sources and effects of the problem and, at the same time, facilitate the release of tension.

Jennifer's Story

Jennifer was a twenty-eight-year-old single high school teacher, who had a history of engaging in intense emotional relationships with men involving sexual activity at a very early stage. These relationships were short-lived and, in spite of Jennifer's efforts to create a deep emotional connection with the man she hoped to keep dating, these men always let her down and broke off their relationship.

Jennifer did not understand the reasons behind her choices and behavior. Several attempts at therapy had not produced much in the way of results, even though she had been given a variety of insight-focused interpretations and explanations about the reasons she kept engaging in such self-destructive behavior.

One day Jennifer saw a videotape about the chaotic life of an artist who had straightened out her life through her painting and drawing. This inspired Jennifer to begin to draw and paint. She came into therapy already aware that there were pent-up tensions within her that were finding expression in her art work. Her therapist avoided asking her direct questions about her feelings, since many of her answers were along the lines of "I don't know what I feel. I'm just upset." Instead, Jennifer talked about the characters she was painting and she described in detail what they were experiencing.

Jennifer was asked to keep a journal in which she would write about her thoughts, feelings, and physical sensations on a daily basis. She was asked to sign her name after each writing. She was told she could write more than once a day providing she noted down the time and date when she wrote.

As she continued to write in her journal, she was instructed to control her urge to act out impulsively whenever she was upset. This was accomplished by instructing her either to sit on her hands for five minutes and meditate and focus on her body sensations, thoughts, and feelings, or to clasp her hands together while meditating and/or focusing on her sensations, thoughts, and feelings.

Sitting *with* her feelings instead of acting out her urges gave her the experience of *containing* her feelings. Later she expressed her feelings in words, by writing in her journal. Then Jennifer was asked to bring her journal to her therapy sessions and to read aloud from her entries. Practicing this discipline empowered her to transform impulses and self-destructive behaviors into written statements, which were later expressed verbally in a supportive environment and reexamined in a healing context.

When Jennifer could find no words to express her urges and impulses, she was instructed to draw or paint. When she found no solace in those activities, she was instructed to cut out pictures from old magazines and words from newspaper headlines and glue them together in a collage that would express what she was feeling and experiencing, without her needing to act out the impulse.

As Jennifer continued practicing self-expression in these new modalities, her self-destructive behaviors began to diminish and eventually disappeared. The urges to act out impulsively were replaced by self-nurturing activities and behaviors, and new relationships that met her needs in a healthy way.

Jennifer's story illustrates a practical solution to distress in the face of uncertainty through the application of safe and satisfying outlets that are more adaptive and self-protective in nature than acting out impulsively or self-destructively.

Exercising the Solution

Make it a habit to keep a personal journal where you regularly review your activities of the day. Write about those activities that caused you to feel distress and those that brought you comfort, those that caused pain, and those that brought you pleasure. Write about activities that made you feel competent and those that made you feel incompetent, those that made you feel helpless and those that made you feel resourceful. Also, write about those activities that made you feel hopeless and those that gave you hope.

As you continue to write on a daily basis, look for patterns and educate yourself about your strengths and weaknesses, assets and liabilities. This mode of self-expression can empower you to use words as a replacement for impulsive actions.

As you write, ask yourself what is the purpose of your life? What are your goals and objectives? What are your values and beliefs? When you establish greater clarity in answering these questions, then ask yourself to what extent do the activities you engage in, as part of your daily living, lead to progress in accomplishing your goals and objectives? To what extent are your activities compatible with your basic, fundamental values and beliefs?

Generally speaking, the more discrepancy there is between what you do and what you believe, the greater the stress you experience. The more the actions of your daily life are compatible and in accord with your basic values and belief systems, the more you experience inner peace and a sense of authenticity.

Stress Needs an Outlet

Some people find a way to express their distress when facing uncertainty by engaging in a variety of aerobic physical exercises. Such physical activities are healthy outlets for your mind and body, confirming the age-old Latin expression, "a sound mind in a sound body" (*mensana in corpore sano*).

This concept is reflected in the definition of stress that states it is *the result of a contradiction between what your body wants to do and what the environment allows you to do.* The requirements of living in civilized society understandably do not allow us to exercise our animal instincts for hunting and fighting, or to exercise our other basic biological urges whenever we feel like doing so. Problems arise because these instincts and urges are genetically and biologically programmed into our bodies. We must control their expression. When we cannot express our instincts to attack those whom we feel are trying to injure us and, most of the time, we cannot, this creates inner tension. That tension must be managed and discharged in safe, healthy, and socially acceptable ways.

Leading a healthy, productive, and balanced lifestyle requires us to find acceptable outlets for our tension and stress. Getting good nutrition, adequate exercise and rest helps us to stay healthy and more capable of managing our stress effectively. Practicing relaxation, centering, and quieting exercises also helps greatly, as does clear, rational thinking and the creative uses of imagination.

The following exercises are designed to help you release tension and externalize physical and emotional discomfort and negative thoughts and feelings. This will help you to achieve calm control over yourself so that you feel totally in charge, and able to handle stressful situations more effectively no matter when or where they occur.

Caution: *The following exercises are never to be done while you are driving or operating dangerous machinery. Note that this caution applies to all of the exercises in this book that involve closing your eyes, tuning into your imagination, and becoming inwardly focused and absorbed.*

The Flow and Discard Technique

This is a simple mind-body exercise that involves using your imagination in a productive way. Begin by feeling and observing the physical tension in your body. Notice where it is most concentrated and intense. Stay with the feelings and sensations of this tension for a while. Now, shift your focus to one of your hands. Imagine the physical tension flowing from its source in your body, down into your arm, and through your arm into the hand you've chosen. Feel the tension flowing, and, as you experience this, tighten that hand into a fist. Make your fist tighter and tighter as more and more tension flows into your hand.

At some point, open your fist and shake out the tension that's accumulated from your hand, or just open your fist and let the tension *flow out* of your fingers and your palm. Repeat these steps as needed, and allow the tension and discomfort to flow out of you. That's all there is to it.

The Silent Emotional and Physical Release Technique

The following exercise is adapted from a method developed by the psychologist Helen Watkins (1997). Imagine yourself walking on a path and coming across a large boulder. This boulder is clearly blocking you from getting to where you want to go. It represents the frustrations that stand in your way. These frustrations keep you from getting what you want.

You stand for a short while staring at this obstacle. Then, conveniently, you see leaning against this boulder a large, unbreakable, thick stick. You pick it up and begin to strike the boulder with it. You hit the boulder again and again with the intent of smashing it to pieces. Eventually, the boulder starts chipping into smaller and smaller bits and finally it breaks apart. After you've pulverized it, you feel tired and sort of drained, but in a healthy, pleasant way.

You walk on a trail into a beautiful meadow, a garden, or any peaceful, safe, and tranquil place. You find a comfortable spot to sit and rest and enjoy the tranquility and peace for a while. You experience pleasant feelings spreading throughout your body. When you are ready, you emerge from this state of imaginative concentration and return to what you were doing in your usual alert and awake state. You feel refreshed, invigorated, and much more relaxed than when you started the exercise.

Journaling and Artistic Expression

It is a healthy and adaptive habit to use a journal to express in words your thoughts, feelings, and physical sensations about your past and present experiences, as well as your fears of the future. However, because there are times when there may be no adequate words to express your feelings and experiences, a useful alternative can be to use pictures you cut from magazines and other print media to make a collage of images that will express how you feel. You can also choose to draw, color, paint, or sculpt your feelings and experiences.

You also may wish to use music therapeutically to experience your feelings of joy, sadness, anger, agitation, and serenity. You can use music to induce a state of mind conducive to hope, inner peace, love, connection, and faith. One specific technique is to record your own audiotape of selected, musical pieces that are meaningful to you to induce a shift in your mind from feeling fearful and vulnerable to feeling strong, confident, and hopeful. You can replay this personal tape whenever you want to and it feels appropriate to do so.

Releasing Muscle Tension Physically

Another exercise solution would be to release the muscle tension that has accumulated inside your body using a physical exercise rather than a visualization. For instance, consider the following case example.

Kevin's Story

Kevin is a forty-three-year-old bus driver. Every workday he is confronted with rudeness, inescapable traffic jams, and noxious fumes. In the past, he frequently became dizzy, nauseated, and had stress headaches because of his job, until one day when he described his physical symptoms to a friend at work. From his friend, an experienced bus driver, he learned a quick and effective method to release tension and regain a sense of serenity.

When he is stuck in traffic, with his hands on the steering wheel, he tenses the muscles in his hands and legs, and then slowly and gradually releases the tension. This release of muscle tension through repetition becomes associated with the experience of calmness and mental tranquility.

Over the years, Kevin also has learned to apply this technique to the muscles of his forehead, face, throat, neck, shoulders, arms, hands, chest, abdomen, back, legs, knees, and feet, basically all over his entire physical body. Doing this exercise has eliminated his aches and pains and prevented the reoccurrence of other physical discomforts.

Breathe Away Stress and Tension

Still another exercise solution for stress and tension is to breathe away both of them. Consider the following case example.

Marianne's Story

Marianne is a thirty-four-year-old single mother who works as waitress. Her job is very stressful, filled with demanding customers, and long hours on her feet. Her life outside of work is also filled with stress and uncertainty. For several years, she made repeated attempts to quit smoking, but was never successful for longer than two weeks. Each time she picked up smoking again she blamed it on the stress of her daily life.

After being diagnosed with chronic bronchitis, Marianne decided it was time to stop smoking for good. She was quite worried about whether she could follow through on her latest vow to quit because she thought that smoking helped her relax. After talking with a friend who had stopped smoking for good, she realized that the habit of smoking actually made her more anxious. So, this time she was determined to succeed.

After taking a yoga class, she learned how to use breathing as a way to release tension. She decided to use a simple breathing exercise to help relieve her frequent tensions and stress.

Whenever she felt her stress levels rise, or she felt a desire for a cigarette, she took four slow, deep breaths instead, inhaling slowly through her nose and exhaling slowly through her mouth. While taking these slow deep breaths, she focused her visual attention on some neutral and absorbing object not too far away. This new habit became a regular coping tool that enabled her to beat the smoking habit for good, and to defuse her stress level before it got too high.

A Solution for Generalized Pain and Fatigue

Situate yourself comfortably in a safe and quiet place where you will not be disturbed for about ten minutes. Sit with your back upright and supported, your hands resting palms down on your thighs, and your feet flat on the floor. Allow your eyes to flutter closed and keep them comfortably closed while you pay attention to your breathing without trying to change your breathing. If your eyelids continue to flutter, this is fine; soon you may not notice it anymore.

As you continue paying attention to your breathing without trying to change it, you will notice your breathing changing all by itself. It may become slower, more rhythmic and regular. You may also notice that you are breathing from your abdomen more than usual. This is a normal, natural, relaxing, and revitalizing way to breathe.

Once you notice these pleasant changes taking place, shift your focus of attention to your head. Beginning with your head, slowly move your attention and awareness down your body, scanning for tension or discomfort. Whenever you notice tension or discomfort in any part of your body, stop there and instruct the tension or discomfort to leave; replace it with calm, comfort, and tranquility.

You may also imagine any physical remedy that might ease the discomfort; for example, strong and gentle massaging hands; a warm pulsating shower or stream of water; a cool stream of water; concentrated pressure on the tender points; tension melting or draining away; a medicinal, healing ointment penetrating deep into your muscles; and so on.

Proceed in this same way down throughout your entire body. Attend to each spot that needs to feel more comfortable. When you finally reach your feet and your toes, imagine tension and discomfort draining out your toes and out of your fingertips with each breath you exhale. End your self-relaxation session by scanning your entire body for any residual, remaining discomfort. Take several slow, deep breaths and exhale away any remaining discomfort.

When your deepest mind (your subconscious) knows that you have reached a level of comfort that is acceptable and makes a positive, noticeable difference, that new comfort level will last for some time after you emerge from your meditative state. Then your eyes will open and come back into focus, and the objects around you become clear in all of their natural beauty—their shape and size in reality. You feel alert, refreshed, energized, relaxed, and much more comfortable for some time after your eyes open and you emerge from your meditation.

Improve Your Tolerance for Frustration

He who has a why to live can bear with almost any how.

—Friedrich Nietzsche

Improve your tolerance for frustration so you can weather any storm. Frustration means not getting what you want or getting what you don't want. It refers to an obstruction that prevents you from reaching your goals. It refers to being hindered or restrained. Unfortunately, frustration is a fact of life. Ever since we humans were thrown out of the Garden of Eden, instant gratification has been a rare event. So, to live a healthy life, you must improve the coping skills that enable you to deal with frustration. This is what we mean by improving your tolerance for frustration.

Frustration tolerance refers to the ability to continue living a balanced, healthy life despite encountering repeated interferences. It refers to how robust you are in the face of life's stressors and challenges. How well you handle frustration forms the basis for how well you cope with uncertainty. When you build strong frustration tolerance skills, you empower yourself to cope more effectively in times of uncertainty.

Chronically facing uncertainty with no resolute strategy for handling it can lead to a state of chronic stress. This is because we have a basic biological need to resolve uncertainty. This need to resolve uncertainty is what motivates new learning experiences. In fact, there is an optimal level of uncertainty. Too much uncertainty may provoke excessive anxiety and tension; too little uncertainty may lead to boredom and indifference.

So, as we shall discuss and illustrate, one key to not becoming worn out by persistent uncertainty is to find ways to moderate the degree of uncertainty that you deal with in your day-to-day living. A second key is to control your anxiety about uncertainty. This key entails learning how to accept and tolerate uncomfortable feelings. We shall address this issue later in this chapter.

Unbound continuing uncertainty extracts a toll on your body. It triggers the "stress response," also called the "fight-flight response." This set of physical and mental reactions to uncertainty, to excessive demands, and to perceived or real threats is actually an adaptive response. It motivates you to reorient yourself in a reflex-like way, so that you can better cope with the stress of uncertainty.

This set of basic responses was necessary for survival in prehistoric times when humans lived in the wild with regular exposure to danger and life-threatening uncertainties. In fact, this fight-flight response continues to be basic to survival. However, when it is excessively or unnecessarily activated, your mind and body wear down.

When the fight-flight stress response continues activating various cascades of hormonal and biochemical changes in your body, even after the reasons for your stress are gone, then you don't get any rest. Eventually you and your body become exhausted from the continual strain. Your body is like a brilliantly designed machine. Without proper tune-ups at appropriate intervals, you are likely to wear it out.

Your brain and body work in harmony together because there is a feedback system of chemical messenger molecules and hormones called *neurotransmitters*. Chronic stress triggers this hormonal-neurotransmitter system to work on overdrive, and eventually it gets worn down. A variety of mental and physical disorders may result.

The neurotransmitter system is a communication system. It exists so that your cells can communicate with each other. It transmits electrical and chemical messages up and down your nervous system, to and from your brain, with the rest of your body. It needs to be well cared for and not to be on "red alert" all the time for your body and mind to function properly.

Chronic states of stress throw this system out of balance. When we are overaroused and anxious most of the time, this may result in certain conditions associated with running continually on overdrive. This may eventually lead to a system slow-down, producing other conditions, such as "burnout" which then may lead to clinical depression.

Moreover, being habitually stressed-out often leads to painful, distressing symptoms such as, insomnia, general fatigue, loss of energy, loss of enthusiasm, impaired concentration, feeling easily distracted, indecisiveness, lapses in judgment, slowed thinking, feeling drained, nervous, and irritable.

A New Way to Think About the Problem

It is very important to understand the feeling of being worn down in a way that leads to an effective solution—that is, a way that helps you to mobilize your energy to cope well with the frustrations and anxiety of uncertainty. Many people explain to themselves that their state of being worn down or burned out is the result of their moral or character weakness.

Some religious people may interpret burnout as meaning they are not strong enough in their faith, or that the burnout is God's way of punishing them for their sins.

It is important to understand that, even though these interpretations may have some merit symbolically, in this context it is more helpful to view the problem in a new way, one that is compatible with the idea of a system that is chemically out of balance. The solution to this problem is to provide our brains and bodies with ample amounts of the vital chemicals they need to function efficiently in carrying out the activities of daily living. These chemicals are a combination of nutrients, vitamins, minerals, and, at times, additional supplements for coping with stress and uncertainty.

Reframing the way we think and feel about a problem is also associated with chemical changes in the brain's and body's neurotransmitters. In other words, your thoughts are like the nutrients that you feed yourself; healthy thoughts are like healthy food, and unhealthy thoughts are the equivalent of junk food.

Practical Solutions

The essence of the solution to the problem of building a healthy tolerance for frustration is to adopt habits that will restore and replenish your brain and your body. Regular practice of these habits will prevent uncertainty from wearing you down.

Your brain and body need to be provided with the proper raw materials to regenerate their cells. Cells don't stay the same over a lifetime. Some cells have a life span of only several weeks, others stay with you for many years. Your cellular chemicals are constantly being rebuilt and regenerated. The raw materials you provide for your cells come in the form of proper nutrition associated with vitamins, minerals, and perhaps supplements. Combined with appropriate physical exercise, sensory and mental stimulation, and adequate rest (especially nighttime sleep) these factors are all key to building and maintaining a healthy tolerance for frustration.

Nutrition

Our brains are made up mostly of essential fats, minerals, protein components (amino acids), and water. To protect and rejuvenate the material holding our brain cells together and providing the insulation for the neurons in the brain, we need the proper raw materials in the form of essential fats, oils, amino acids, and minerals. In the past twenty years, we have become more aware of the vital importance of essential fats in our diet because our bodies are not able to produce these particular fats on their own. We have learned that totally fat-free diets are not only unhelpful to the brain, they can actually cause damage. New research promotes the idea of a "smart-fat diet" rather than a "fat-free diet" (Schmidt 2001).

These essential fats are Omega-3 (alpha-linolenic acid) and Omega-6 (linoleic acid). The typical American diet is very rich in Omega-6 fats and rather poor in Omega-3. However, it is the Omega-3 that the brain needs most for optimal function and operation. The Mediterranean and the traditional Asian Pacific Rim nations' diets are rich in Omega-3 fats, and the ratio of Omega-3 to Omega-6 is in favor of Omega-3. Foods rich in Omega-3 include nuts and seeds such as almonds, walnuts, pecans, pumpkin seeds, flax seeds, soybeans, and wheat germ, as well as linseed oil, and cold water ocean fish like mackerel, salmon, tuna, and halibut.

Your diet should be balanced with an ample supply of essential fats, proteins, and carbohydrates. Protein-rich foods are a source of amino acids, the building blocks of new cells. Carbohydrate-rich foods are a source of energy-rich fuel, but too much carbohydrate in your diet can turn into storage fats, which put a strain on your heart, pancreas, and liver.

There are many different diets, each one claiming to offer the best dietary solution to achieve a long and healthy life. How can all of these different diets provide the best answer for you? The truth is they can't. There is simply no universal, best diet for everyone.

Different diets dictate different ratios or balances between proteins, carbohydrates, and fats. Although this is not a book devoted to diets or nutrition, we believe that it is important to recognize that the balance of water with vitamins, minerals, and essential nutrients (proteins, carbohydrates, and fats) in your diet is best determined by taking into account a combination of factors. These include: how sedentary or active your lifestyle is, your body type, and the climate in which you live

In addition, your medical health condition, family history, and genetic predisposition to certain diseases (such as hypertension and heart disease) should be factored in to your total assessment. So, just following a diet taken from a book is not enough and, indeed, may be harmful. Competent, individualized medical supervision and nutritional counseling by qualified licensed health professionals is essential. Finding the right diet for *you* can be a complex pursuit. Yet, there are some definite concepts about proper nutrition that we know apply almost universally.

Most diet experts agree that you should be careful to reduce and, at times, totally avoid processed foods, which contain high amounts of sugar, salt, saturated fats, and unhealthy trans-fatty acids, as well as many chemical preservatives designed to lengthen their shelf life. Eating simple, unprocessed foods is healthier and better for your body and brain. Also, it is usually a good idea to add a daily multivitamin and mineral supplement, as well as ample sources of Omega-3 essential fats, to your daily diet.

Olive oil is an excellent source of mono-unsaturated fats. These fats serve as building blocks for neurons. In addition, olive oil contains antioxidants and two chemicals, squalene and oleic acid. Together, these chemicals inhibit the rapid oxidation and breakdown of essential fats into harmful by-products called free radicals that speed up the biological aging process.

Some people supplement their daily food intake with additional amounts of Omega-3 fish oil capsules. Some people take additional amounts of vitamin E to improve circulation, antioxidant activity (the removal of destructive free radicals), and fat and cholesterol metabolism. Some people also take supplements with additional doses of vitamin C. Vitamin C is a powerful antioxidant which the body needs in higher amounts during times of stress and anxiety.

Dr. Linus Pauling, the Nobel Prize Laureate biochemist, strongly advocated taking high doses of vitamin C during times of stress. He believed that this strengthens the immune system and provides a vital booster to many biochemical processes essential for the production of neurotransmitters and hormones.

One of the functions of Vitamin B6 is to promote healthy nerve transmission. It is the source of an enzyme that serves as an important mediator of many neurochemical processes. Therefore, because the nerves are the body's information highway, B6 is necessary for intercellular communication.

In summary, the brain needs an adequate supply of the above-mentioned essential chemicals to handle frustration optimally.

Sensory Stimulation

For the brain to function properly, it also needs to have the right amount of sensory stimulation in the form of light, sound, touch, smell, and taste. There is an old saying from the Hebrew Talmud: "Pretty sights, pleasant sounds, and sweet scents keep a man healthy." This indicates that even thousands of years ago, scholars knew what it took to keep the brain operating in top condition. It is well known that when the brain and body are deprived of all sensory input, the subject experiences an altered state of mind marked by anxiety, physiological distress, and mental distortions, such as hallucinations and delusions.

A very important concept here is the understanding that keeping the brain working in optimal condition helps to maintain a state of mind associated with images of good health and wellness, serenity, peace, and prosperity. States of mind are manifested in the body. When your brain is in a state of anxiety, fear, or stress, your body's physiology matches your mental state through the influence of your autonomic nervous system (the tiny nerves that regulate the function of your internal organs and blood vessels). This is also done by the secretion of various hormones from the pituitary gland and from the hypothalamus. Hormones from other glands also influence the body to reflect specific states of mind. When the brain operates in a state of calm and inner peace, the body matches the mental state with a relaxation response, reducing blood pressure, optimizing heart rate and breathing, and creating peace and tranquility in the lungs, muscles, intestines, immune system, and elsewhere.

Getting an optimal level of positive mental stimulation can keep you from becoming worn down by uncertainty and stress. It is important to remember this when you are faced with uncertainty. In most people, no uncertainty at all will almost certainly lead to boredom after a short period of time. Their brains become dulled with trivial, routine habits and mindless activities. On the other hand, coping with uncertainty in an adaptive and functional manner, as we are teaching you to do, will ensure that your brain is getting enough mental stimulation to keep it functioning optimally in dealing with uncertainty.

Mental Attitude

The right mental attitude can save you from being worn down by persistent uncertainty. What is that attitude? It is an outlook that accepts uncertainty as a permanent part of life, and is associated with the satisfaction of keeping a cool head in emergencies. It is an outlook that celebrates past successes and remembers them when facing new problems. It is an attitude that knows good things are worth working hard for, or fighting for, if necessary. It is the outlook that knows that Rome wasn't built in a single day. It accepts frustration and uncertainty about ultimate outcomes as part of the excitement and stimulation of living. It accepts problems as new puzzles in need of solutions, reframes adversities as new challenges, and views crises as opportunities for transformation and self-renewal.

This attitude avoids making absolute demands; it transforms *demands* into *preferences*. When you have this attitude, it enables you to distinguish between what you *want* and what you *need*. We *need* water, food, and shelter to live. We *prefer* to live comfortably.

The key to establishing and maintaining such an attitude is to avoid extreme thinking as much as possible. With few exceptions, life is lived in shades of gray rather than in black and white. When we get caught up in thinking in extremes, or in all-or-nothing ways, we get stuck in rigidity and we deprive ourselves of the flexibility we need to cope with uncertainty. So, we want to cultivate the mental attitude of flexibility rather than rigidity (see chapter 10 for more on this subject).

The right mental attitude for optimal coping with uncertainty views it as our responsibility to handle it in healthy, flexible, and productive ways. That is, it views our reactions to times of uncertainty as within our control, and not controlled by external circumstances, or by the winds of chance. The right mental attitude holds that we can be masters of our own destiny.

United States Senator John McCain (1999) tells how having the "right mental attitude" helped him to endure the extreme hardships of psychological torture and physical abuse in his five and a half years of imprisonment during the Vietnam War. Like Victor Frankl, the Jewish psychiatrist who survived unbelievable horrors in Nazi death camps during World War II (1959), the then-young naval aviator John McCain relied on his ability to choose and set his own *inner* attitude during horrific *external* circumstances. He writes that this was the one "freedom" his captors and tormentors could not take away from him, unless *he* gave it up.

Senator McCain's story illustrates how the "right mental attitude" builds tolerance for frustration and strength in the face of the greatest of hardships.

Anxiety Tolerance and Mindfulness

The right mental attitude leads you to experience your feelings rather than avoid them. One of the most powerful keys for coping with uncertainty in a healthy way is to learn to tolerate uncomfortable feelings like anxiety, fear, anger, frustration, disappointment, sadness, guilt, envy, shame, and embarrassment. The strategy of *mindfulness* can assist in this task.

Basically, mindfulness means staying in the present with what you are feeling. It means being aware and conscious of your current experience, and allowing yourself to feel your feelings without making self-deprecating judgments for having those feelings. To change your feelings you must acknowledge that you have them in the first place. It is hard or impossible to change that which you do not acknowledge exists.

Another important point is that you will feel better if you acknowledge the following distinctions: One distinction is between the initial step of acknowledging a feeling and the second step of containing the feeling and not letting it control and run your behavior. Destructive feelings can be changed by changing your thoughts.

Another useful distinction to make is between what you think about and feel, and how you act. The point here is that you can experience feelings and thoughts associated with undesirable behaviors, and do something about changing these feelings and thoughts, as long as you do not act them out in reality.

It has been said that "all things must pass." We would add that no feeling lasts forever. This recognition makes it easier to manage the anxiety associated with not knowing what will happen (uncertainty) because it reminds us that the anxiety and discomfort are temporary. So, it is useful to tell yourself that you *can* tolerate and handle uncomfortable feelings and you can get through difficult, uncertain times in your life. See the "Exercising the Solution" section below, for an exercise that can help you learn to master your uncomfortable feelings.

Proper Rest

It is well known that sleep deprivation prevents the brain from functioning adequately in dealing with the demands of daily life. When people are sleep deprived for several days, they begin to show signs of brain dysfunction. These signs may include persistent aches and pains, hallucinations, paranoia, poor judgment, cognitive distortions, impulsive behavior, irritability, lowered frustration tolerance, memory impairment, and difficulties in learning new material.

In natural, restorative sleep, the brain shifts into a different operating mode. In this mode, various healing chemicals are produced and different systems of the brain become active, while other systems rest and become revitalized. This mode of natural sleep has been recorded with EEG (electroencephalographs) measurements of brain waves, which distinguish between REM (rapid eye movement) and non-REM sleep, each of which is a different phase of unconscious brain processing. The REM phase involves dreaming and the non-REM does not. Dreaming is an essential, brain rejuvenating, unconscious activity that takes place during REM sleep. Prevention of REM sleep causes daytime drowsiness and mental fogginess.

A good night's sleep that goes through several cycles of REM and non-REM sleep recharges your brain adequately and prepares it for optimal functioning during your daytime waking state. A good night's sleep is associated with waking up in the morning feeling well-rested and energized to face the new day's challenges. A disrupted night's sleep is associated with waking up in the morning feeling tired and less able to cope.

There are certain habits associated with getting a good night's sleep. These are referred to as "healthy sleep hygiene."

The following is a list of behaviors and habits associated with healthy sleep hygiene:

- Establish a regular bedtime.

- Stick to this time seven days a week.

- Sleep in the same room and same bed every night, when you are at home.

- Establish a bedtime ritual (e.g., brushing your teeth, removing your makeup, emptying your bladder, putting on nighttime attire, etc.).

- Get up at the same time every morning seven days a week

- Establish a reliable wake-up routine (e.g., music, sunlight, a partner's gentle nudge).

- Make sure your bedroom is used only for sleep or sexual intimacy (avoid using your bedroom as a workplace or dining room).

- Avoid stimulating activities in the bedroom and before sleep (like watching TV, eating, listening to the news, arguing or discussing conflicts).

- Avoid stimulating foods or chemicals before sleep (like caffeine, nicotine, etc.). Also, avoid eating heavy meals before bedtime.

- Sleep in loose-fitting, comfortable clothing. Avoid sleeping in tight nightwear.

- Engage in activities that allow you to shift gears and wind down (e.g., listen to relaxing music or relaxation tapes, do a relaxation exercise, read light, inspirational, or amusing material).

- Prepare your bed with clean sheets, blankets, and pillows for comfort.

- Some people find it helpful to say a prayer as part of their bedtime ritual.

Exercising the Solution

Caution: *The following exercises are to be practiced only in safe and appropriate places. Never do these exercises while driving a car or operating machinery.*

A Self-Centering Exercise. The following self-centering exercise will help you to counter extreme, all-or-nothing thinking in situations that test the limits of your tolerance for frustration.

Read the following statement to yourself several times. Meditate on it for a few moments.

> *Don't judge yourself on the basis of where you are now, but rather in terms of where you have come from, and how far you have traveled to get where you are now.*

Sit in a comfortable position in a private place. Take several deep breaths and activate the state of calm relaxation. Allow yourself to get in touch with the logical, rational, mature part of your brain. It is this part of your brain that is capable of seeing the world around you and in you as a whole, taking into account all the different factors and ingredients that affect your life at the present time. It is this part of your brain that holds the wisdom and knowledge of your past, memories of your family, and the circumstances of your life in the past. It holds the memories of the significant events in your childhood. It knows how far you have come to be where you are today. It also knows your desires and dreams, your strengths and limitations. It knows to take into account the future and all of the promises the future holds for you. It can assess and evaluate what is truly in your best interest as you evaluate your current situation.

Listen to this part of your brain. It can show you the wisdom of being flexible with yourself. And whenever you hear your critical inner voice attacking you for not getting an A in the exam you took, or not getting the promotion you wanted, listen to your other inner voice of wisdom and allow it to reveal to you other possibilities and explanations before you jump to self-defeating conclusions. Now say the following affirmation to yourself:

> *I am a human being and like all human beings I am not perfect. Imperfection is a part of human nature. I am entitled to feel any feelings that are part of the full range of human emotions. Even though I am not perfect, I can still do much good in my life and continue to aspire to improve myself as I grow emotionally and intellectually. I deserve a great deal of credit for giving myself the courage to be flexible, adaptable, and kind to myself.*

Now take several deep breaths and let your eyes open. Allow yourself to feel alert, fully awake, and refreshed.

A Cognitive Exercise. This next cognitive exercise will help you to counter extreme, all-or-nothing thinking in trying situations.

Remember the last time things didn't go your way. What did you tell yourself? Is it possible that you told yourself something like, "I can never do anything right." "I am a real jerk." "I always come last." "I never win"? Now, look forward to the next time you face a challenge or an adversity. Imagine coming up against various obstacles that block you from attaining your goal. As you imagine these obstacles, let your inner critic sound off. However, as it does this, practice answering your inner critic's insults, dire predictions, complaints, overgeneralizations, and putdowns.

Ask your inner critic whether such words as "never," "always," and so on are true. Ask it if there have ever been any exceptions. Search your memory for those exceptions and come up with answers to put your inner critic in its place.

Also, remember the last time that you worked hard to get something that you eventually got. Recall how, at times, you were in the dark and were unsure about how things would turn out. Remember the times when you might have felt like throwing in the towel and giving up. Because eventually you did get what you were seeking or hoping for, you now know that you did not give up and that you did cope with whatever hardships or frustrations were in your way.

Now, think about something you are working toward getting in the future. Bring to mind some of the obstacles, annoyances, and frustrations that you are likely to encounter or have already encountered in this particular journey. Remind yourself of some of the similarities between these frustrations and the past frustrations that you did manage to cope with successfully. Tell yourself that you will cope with these current adversities as successfully as those you coped with in the past.

Now just sit quietly for a few minutes and pay attention to your breathing without trying to change it in any way. Permit yourself to settle down and relax. You may wish to do this with your eyes closed or with your eyes open. You may wish to bring to mind one of your victories to enjoy, or you may wish to simply maintain a blank mind. When you are ready, blink your eyes several times and come back to your normal, alert, awake focus.

A Mindfulness Exercise. The following mindfulness exercise can help in building tolerance for anxiety and other uncomfortable feelings.

Take a deep breath and, as you exhale, recall and become mindful of a recent situation in which your patience and your tolerance for frustration were tested. Perhaps you were rushing to an important appointment for which you were late, and you got stuck in unexpected traffic; or perhaps you were extremely angry with somebody; or perhaps you were afraid that something dreadful might happen. Whatever it was, ask yourself if the problem was resolved. Did you get through it? Did you solve the problem eventually? Did you survive?

The fact that you are here now, reading our book, suggests that you did get through it. Now, think of some current unresolved problem or source of frustration. Whatever it is, sit with the feelings that come up as you think about it for a little while. Allow your feelings and thoughts to continue to emerge and give yourself permission to experience them. Let them flow. As you do this, you feel more in charge.

The feelings do not harm you. In fact, as you experience them, notice that their intensity and quality may begin to change. In this exercise, the goal is to sit with your feelings for a little while.

Do this exercise several times a day for five to ten minutes at a time. Repeating it will help you to become hardier and more resilient in the face of uncomfortable feelings. Do this exercise as soon as possible after the emergence of unpleasant feelings. You will soon find yourself practicing this new awareness in different life situations as you build your tolerance for frustration. As you do this, you get better and better at tolerating frustration and getting through uncomfortable feelings with greater comfort. Experience this for yourself. You may be pleasantly surprised.

A Restful Relaxation Break. During the times of the day when you are aware that you are feeling tired, run down, or just know you need a rest, take that rest using the following method.

First, find a comfortable place to sit with your hands on your lap, your back supported, and your feet flat on the floor.

Now, you are ready to take a relaxing break, so just rest back and relax for a little while. Close your eyes and allow yourself to relax now. Soon you feel much more relaxed, very relaxed. You can take a little time for yourself now. Feel free.

You can enjoy this restful time for yourself even more by paying attention to your breathing without trying to change it. If your mind wanders, the moment you realize that you are thinking of something else, bring your mind back to focus on your breathing, and feel yourself going deeper into relaxation. You feel more deeply relaxed with each breath you take.

As you go deeper and deeper into restful relaxation with each breath, the doorway to your subconscious mind opens.

You now have the opportunity to talk with your subconscious and discover what you need to know to rejuvenate and revitalize yourself. So, when you open your eyes and awaken, you feel refreshed, reenergized, invigorated, restored, and yet relaxed at the same time.

Or, you need not talk at all. You can simply rest and relax easily and comfortably until you are ready to awaken feeling reinvigorated, refreshed, and relaxed. Doing this exercise for several minutes at those times during the day when you're feeling stressed helps you to avoid feeling worn down. Regular practice of this exercise helps you stay rested and calm.

It is so simple. When you sit down, close your eyes, and pay attention to your breathing, without trying to change your breathing, you have done it. That's all there is to it!

As long as it is safe and appropriate to do so, and you are not driving or operating any machinery, from now on, you can close your eyes, and take one or two slow deep breaths, whenever you are ready to feel more relaxed. When you do, you know what it feels like to tap into your brain's natural ability to take a break and rejuvenate itself. When you just pay attention to your breathing, you enjoy how nice it feels to be able to relax instantly for a short while, until you are ready to return to your regular business of the day.

By practicing this technique in this way, you function more efficiently and feel more rested throughout the day because you observe and honor the natural rhythms of your brain and body.

Develop Healthy Self-Acceptance

We are what we imagine ourselves to be.

—Kurt Vonnegut, Jr.

Develop healthy self-acceptance because you owe it to yourself. There are times when uncertainty about the future is associated with feelings of helplessness and incompetence. This happens particularly following an event for which we feel a sense of responsibility that resulted in failure, pain, or loss. That sense of helplessness is sometimes coupled with a feeling of disappointment in ourselves for not solving or preventing the problems arising from the unfortunate event.

Thoughts about the future become associated with uncertainty, coupled with fears that more of the same will happen again, and that we have no power to prevent the unfortunate event from reoccurring. This can lead to a loss of trust in yourself and an increase in anxiety or sadness that may lead to depression.

Clinical depression is associated with low self-esteem and feelings of hopelessness. At times, shame and humiliation creep in too, and the person who is depressed withdraws from the outside world. This reduces that person's social interactions with family members, friends, and coworkers.

On the surface, the person appears to be quieter, and does not initiate any activities to create pleasure, fun, or a sense of mastery. Instead, the depressed person engages only in the absolutely necessary actions of daily living, and those activities are done in a rote manner, without any joy. This loss of the ability to experience joy is very common in depressed people; it is called *anhedonia*.

Clinical depression is a condition that requires professional help. It is important that the depressed individual see a qualified licensed health care professional as soon as possible.

When someone becomes depressed, that person's "internal critic" becomes harsh and unforgiving. When this happens, the depressed person feels the weight of this inner critic's condemnation. This leads to feeling even more beaten down and hopeless, and in severe cases, the person becomes immobilized and many require treatment in a hospital setting.

However, it is important to understand that at one time or another everyone experiences some form of internal self-criticism. The point at which this turns into clinical depression is defined by the severity and duration of dysfunction with the activities of daily living.

A New Way to Think About the Problem

Depressive states in human beings can be viewed as a remnant of old, biological, wired-in, behavioral responses from our mammalian brain. You are probably familiar with the phenomenon of biological hibernation that occurs in some mammals during the winter season. In the wild, when days are shorter, temperatures drop, sunlight is scarce, and food supplies become meager, animals that hibernate pass the winter in a resting state. In this state, metabolic functions slow down markedly. A typical example is the American black bear who withdraws into safe places like caves, where it hibernates and is able to survive with minimal energy expenditure. The bear wakes up in the spring when there is more sunlight, warmer temperatures, vegetation and other sources of food become abundant, once again.

Human beings have a wired-in response similar to hibernation. This response is called *conservation withdrawal*. It is designed to conserve energy by causing the individual to withdraw from what is perceived as a stressful and potentially dangerous environment. It is basically designed to preserve the organism's life. Depression may be viewed as a form of temporarily retreating into the self to conserve energy and to replenish internal resources in short supply. However, unlike the bear, human beings have an internal observer. When this behavior of conservation withdrawal (depression) fails to meet personal goals and interferes with performing the activities of daily living, it is often experienced as a form of personal failure. The failure messages arrive as thoughts or internal voices from what some have called the "harsh inner critic."

In this new way of viewing depression, it is important to remember that retreating into the self and away from the burdens and stimulation of daily living has been recognized as necessary in human lives and communities for many centuries. In fact, our society has ritualized the need for such retreats. For example, in the military, it is referred to as "R and R" (rest and relaxation). In civilian life, universities give tenured faculty time off called a *sabbatical*. And, in most work settings, employers provide paid vacation time for their employees as part of their benefits package. This, too, is an example of the recognition of the importance of such a retreat.

The solutions that follow are based on the theory that depression may be a biologically programmed message wired into the old mammalian brain. Instead of fighting this message and calling our behavior "lazy," "crazy," "sick," "hopeless," "helpless," "bad," "weak," or other self-blaming names, we can adopt a new view.

That is, we can understand depressive behaviors as natural responses designed to enhance self-protection and self-preservation. In other words, we may just need to take a rest for self-renewal. Unfortunately, people often fight their body's natural needs and drive themselves to their breaking points. This only makes the situation worse and may contribute to a state of self-alienation and clinical depression with even more self-blame, intense guilt, and impaired functioning in the basic activities of daily living.

Healthy self-acceptance refers to the recognition that we have value just because we exist. It does not depend upon how well we do. It is logical and functional to rate our actions. However, it is not logical or functional to rate ourselves as a totality. We exist and that is a fact. What we do with our existence is an open story that we continually create and modify as we live our lives and interpret our experiences. It is not logical, functional, or useful to base our *entire* self-worth on how we rate our actions or performances. Yet, it is a natural, biologically wired-in human tendency to make global evaluations. That includes globally evaluating ourselves. So, how can we resolve this conflict?

The answer is twofold. It encompasses both a cognitive as well as a biological or physical solution. Cognitively, the solution lies in being able to accept ourselves as imperfect, and just judge our actions, rather than ourselves as a totality or whole. It also lies in being able to respond to our inner critics. However, to be able to do this, it is first necessary to recognize and conform to some basic biological needs that we have as humans.

Healthy self-acceptance depends on recognizing that, as humans, we have a biologically wired-in mechanism that causes us to regularly experience periods during the day when our alertness slows down. This requires that we periodically take breaks from our activities to replenish our entire living organism, including our brain. This cyclic phenomenon has been referred to as biological rhythms (Rossi 1991). Rather than fighting these basic biological rhythms, it is healthier to accept them as constituting a protective, self-preserving mechanism, to internalize this mechanism, adjust it, and make the best of it.

Practical Solutions

The essence of the solution to this problem is to create a reasonable response to the internal, critical, harsh, and rigid voice. This response must be designed to reduce feelings of guilt, self-blame, helplessness, and incompetence.

When your internal critic beats you down, you need a counterresponse. The solutions provided here will help you in defining and executing appropriate counterresponses. Jane's story provides an excellent example of how this is done.

Jane's Story

Jane is a forty-eight-year-old emergency medical technician serving in a first responder ambulance squad in a large American city. Following a series of incidents in which she was unable to save the lives of several people severely injured in car accidents, she began to feel sadder and sadder, with thoughts of self-doubt, associated with feelings of guilt, helplessness, and a lack of self-confidence. She said that, at times, she felt listless, tired, and irritable.

She began thinking that the injured people might have been saved if only she had been quicker and more effective in her interventions. She became more unsure about the future and worried about what any day might bring, in terms of similar events. She also noted that she had not had a vacation for more than three years, and had not taken any time off from work.

In the past, Jane had learned the use of activating self-talk to control her harsh inner critic—the voice of a tyrant. So, she went back and reread the book that taught her how to respond to her inner critic and to her negative thoughts about herself. Her new counterresponse sounded something like this:

> *Come on, Jane, you know that you are a well-trained and experienced EMT. Over your many years of working, you have saved hundreds of lives. You have attended many seminars for continuing medical education. Your knowledge is up-to-date, and you are proficient at the most advanced life-saving techniques in emergency medicine. The symptoms you are feeling now are just a sign that you need to take some time off; you need a vacation . . . You need a rest. In fact, Jane, your boss has told you several times in the past year that it would be good for you to start using the many days of your accumulated vacation time. Why don't you take some time off to go to your favorite vacation spot? You know how good this was for you in the past. Even though it was a long time ago, you are able to still remember how much you enjoyed it, how rejuvenating it was for your body, mind, and spirit. And, besides, you have worked so hard the past couple of years; you have earned it and you are worthy of it. You deserve it.*

Jane put these ideas into action quickly by booking a flight to her favorite vacation spot. That activity in and of itself produced some partial relief to her depressed mood and the symptoms associated with it.

Preventing and Bouncing Back from Depression

Psychologists and psychiatrists have developed a form of therapy and a self-help tool called cognitive-behavior therapy, or CBT, that is easy to learn to use and apply to control your "inner critic" (Beck 1976; Ellis 2001). *Cognitive* stands for thinking and *behavior* stands for actions. So, CBT is all about how to change your negative, dysfunctional thoughts and behaviors in order to modify your feelings and make them more positive. Using the CBT tool is simple and this can help you prevent or bounce back from depression.

The basic premise of CBT is that when we become upset and experience feelings of depression, helplessness, and incompetence, it is because of unchecked, negative, self-blaming thoughts. So, the "cure" is to learn to identify and change such thoughts. According to CBT experts, it's as simple as ABC. In fact, the letters A, B, and C stand for the three stages leading to feelings of upset and depression.

The letter "A" stands for the *Activating* event: this is the situation that you are upset about. For example, you may feel incompetent and depressed after failing an important examination, or after failing to accomplish an important task soon enough or well enough.

The letter "B" stands for your *Beliefs* about the *Activating* event; that is, what you think of or tell yourself about what the disappointment or uncertainty means to you or *about* you. It is how you interpret the event or situation. For example, if you tell yourself that you are either a success or a failure and that there is nothing in between, then you are likely to see most things as either successes or failures. This called "all-or-nothing thinking."

The letter "C" stands for the emotional and behavioral Consequences that result from the situation and your beliefs about the situation. These may include feeling helpless and incompetent. Some behaviors associated with these "C's" may include withdrawal, making self-derogatory remarks, crying a lot, overworking, or punishing yourself.

Extreme, reactive, and all-or-nothing thinking can take much of the joy out of life because average performances will not count, and when you perform poorly, you will blame yourself. You then may tend to drive yourself too hard, so that you can succeed at all costs, but you are likely to have difficulty relaxing. You also may tend not to take pleasure or feel mastery when doing things. When you believe that only the end result matters, you may drive yourself and others very harshly. When you engage in all-or-nothing thinking, you are also likely to be a perfectionist. However, no human is perfect because everyone, even the most successful and brightest, make mistakes.

The redeeming value of mistakes is that most mistakes can be corrected. Most of the time, we can back up and fix the problem. When we use all-or-nothing thinking and call something a failure, that is extreme and may be a misnomer. Based on such faulty logic, we are unlikely to think that we can correct the mistake because, after all, it is a failure! Now, let's look at an example of how CBT works in action.

Julie's Story

Julie was a forty-six-year-old special education teacher who had been experiencing job burnout. Over the past several years, she had begun to feel incompetent and helpless at her job. She felt that every year the students in her classes became more and more difficult to manage and teach.

She had begun to think that she did not have the skills to teach these students, despite the fact that she had worked successfully at her job for more than twenty years! When fights between students broke out in her classroom, she wondered if she was responsible because of not having exercised enough control. She worried whether she would be able to break up such fights. She also worried that her students didn't respect her.

She had started feeling more and more uncertain about her future as a teacher, and wondered whether she would be able to put in the ten more years she needed to teach to become eligible for retirement.

Julie was scheduled to be observed teaching her class by her principal. As the days drew close to the principal's visit to her classroom, she found herself feeling more and more anxious. This was because every difficulty she encountered led her to the immediate thought that it would happen again while her class and her teaching style were being observed, and that she would not be able to handle it. Julie told herself that she just could not stand these uncertainties any longer. Her thoughts included worrying about how the teachers' aides and the other teachers viewed her, given the many difficulties she was having with her students.

As a result of her anxieties about all of this uncertainty, she was not sleeping or eating well, and she was irritable and moody. She told herself that if she received a bad evaluation, it would prove her incompetence. Her worries grew so intense that she decided to seek help. With her therapist, she worked out a plan to help her deal more effectively with her uncertainties and to help her bounce back from feeling depressed, helpless, and incompetent.

Her therapist taught her to focus on her beliefs and her self-talk (the B's). He explained to her that it was not the Activating events (i.e., the unruly students, the lack of support in her classroom, and the upcoming observation) that were upsetting her, but rather her Beliefs about these things; that is, what she was telling herself. Her therapist helped her to realize that when she told herself that she was helpless, she felt helpless; and that when she told herself that she was incompetent, she felt incompetent. He helped her to realize that, by telling herself she was a failure, she made herself feel like a failure.

Julie understood this. Then she remembered that she had handled rougher situations on many occasions in the past, and had succeeded in gaining control over her classroom in the face of many previous daunting events. She remembered helping some students achieve better academic and social skills, and feeling good about herself. In fact, she recalled that she had learned in graduate school, and had been told by one of her past principals, that no teacher could help every student.

Julie started to make a habit of responding to her negative automatic self-condemning thoughts with positive self-affirmations. She began to understand that her negative moods and her anxiety about uncertainty were the result of the thoughts she had been thinking and accepting as true without questioning them. She learned how to question and counter such negative thoughts.

When the day of the principal's visit to her classroom came around, she was ready. She had prepared herself. She told herself that she could only do her best, and that was good enough. She promised herself that she would refuse to let the students' behavior or her evaluation make her feel depressed or incompetent. She also told herself that she was resourceful, and that being so was the opposite of being helpless.

The observation session went surprisingly well. Her students behaved better than they had in a while. Nevertheless, her principal was unnecessarily critical of her teaching style. However, instead of thinking negative self-derogatory thoughts after receiving the principal's critical evaluation, Julie told herself that her principal was being unrealistic (which he was), and that she wouldn't get upset over the principal's comments. She could have predicted what he would write. But she had done the best that she could and her students had been fairly well-behaved. She reasoned there was no point in putting herself down.

This marked a turning point for Julie. She began to build up her own confidence and to see her students as challenges, as opposed to obstacles. As long as she did her best and stayed on top of her thinking processes (her *Beliefs* or B's), she no longer felt helpless or incompetent.

Exercising the Solution

The essence of the solution to this problem is to create a response to your internal, critical, harsh, and rigid inner voice. This response is designed to reduce your feelings of guilt, self-blame, helplessness, and incompetence.

As you read this section, you may wish to implement an exercise that allows you to learn the principles of the solution by experiencing the solution through doing. Make it a habit to keep a personal journal in which you write down any thoughts, feelings, and new ideas that you experience on a day-to-day basis. These thoughts, feelings, and ideas are typically triggered by some event in the external world, or by a memory of an event from the past.

When you feel helpless, irritable, incompetent, worried, and so forth, sit down and take a deep breath. First record your spontaneous, negative thoughts and feelings in your journal. Then, slowly exhale and write the following affirmation exercise:

I [your full name] *am a human being and like all human beings, I'm entitled to experience a full range of human emotions such as joy and pleasure, sadness and fear, wonder and boredom, anger and serenity, peace and turmoil, and many more. Emotions are part of my human existence, and I know that I have experienced many feelings throughout my life. However, I am not my feelings. I am much more than that.*

All human beings have thoughts. Some are pleasant and some are painful. Some thoughts are filled with hope for the future and some are filled with despair. Some thoughts are creative and others are dull. As a human being, I, too, have all sorts of thoughts. Some are self-critical and others are self-affirming. However, I must always remember

*that even though I have many thoughts, and even
though some thoughts may be unpleasant and
painful, I am not my thoughts. I am much more
than that.*

*I believe in the essence of life. I believe that I
am connected to a Higher Power. A Higher Power
that fills the world with goodness and hope. I believe
that all humans are imperfect. I believe that since I
am a human being, I, too, am far from being
perfect. However, I know I am good, and I know I
can continue to strive to be better in the ways I live
my life in the present.*

*When I am alone or in the company of others,
my mind becomes more clear and my thoughts are
more focused. My feelings are more positive. My
body works closely with my mind activating ancient
healing wisdom throughout all of my tissues and
cells as I move forward on my journey of healing
and getting well.*

*I know now that I am worthy of being alive. I
know that life is inherently good and I learn to
appreciate the wonders and magic of life in my
day-to-day living experience. I learn to appreciate
acts of kindness for other human beings, and as I
give kindness to others, I learn to receive kindness
when it is given to me.*

*Even when times of uncertainty make me feel
uncomfortable, hopeless, or helpless, I know that
these feelings are temporary, and I know that my
essence goes beyond my feelings of the moment. I
am strong and resilient. I can bounce back to full
energy, strength, vigor, and productive functioning in
my day-to-day life.*

Writing this exercise in your journal will enhance your
self-esteem and make you feel none of a connected member of

your community. Read this statement that you have just written in your journal to yourself. Consider recording it on audiotape so you can play it back at home with your headphones and listen to your voice reading it. Repeated listening to this message will enhance your sense of well-being and your positive mood.

Learn to Forgive

*He who is slow to anger is better than the
mighty; and he who rules his spirit than he who
takes a city.*

—Proverbs 16:32

Learn to forgive yourself and others, and set yourself free.
Anger is a normal reaction when things happen that we think
were intentionally designed to hurt us. We can feel angry at
others, ourselves, life as a whole, and even at God. The problem is that continuing to feel angry doesn't help us to cope
better. It hinders our coping abilities and serves to isolate us by
alienating ourselves and others. Anger may be contagious. So,
when we are continuously angry, we tend to bring that out in
others. Anger alone does not solve problems. It creates new
ones.

There are times when facing uncertainty that the major
feelings which come up are anger and resentment. These feelings are often experienced consciously in the body as a hot sensation in the head, a tightness in the chest, a tight jaw, or

clenched fists. Some people describe the feeling as, "I felt my blood was boiling with anger." Others say, "My eyes saw red." Sometimes angry feelings arise as a result of difficulties in handling uncertainty and the unknown, but these feelings remain unconscious. In those instances, the person may not be aware that he or she is angry, but may nevertheless experience bodily symptoms that result from continued and unrecognized physiological arousal.

You might ask, "What is it about uncertainty that leads to anger and resentment?" Part of the answer may lie in your basic belief about uncertainty. As discussed in chapter 1, one of the problems facing some people who are struggling to stay calm in the face of uncertainty is the belief that uncertainty should not be a part of life. When you believe that something shouldn't be a problem, but nevertheless it is, there is a natural tendency to feel annoyed. Now, here's the rub. If you just feel annoyed about having to face uncertainty, then the experience of dealing with the fact of uncertainty is not likely to lead you to anger. However, if that annoyance is coupled with the *demand* that your goals or need-gratification *must not be frustrated*, then you are likely to experience more than just annoyance when your goals are not met. Your annoyance is likely to transform into anger and resentment.

Anger and resentment are a person's response to not having his or her needs met, coupled with the belief that those needs *must* be met, and the belief that their failure to be met is someone's *fault*. The point is that anger arises only when there is someone to blame. That someone may be someone else or yourself. So, you can be angry at others or angry at yourself. When you are angry at yourself, that often leads to depression. In fact, psychiatrists often describe depression as anger turned inward. This is accurate.

When you are angry at someone else, that may lead to hostility or aggressive behavior because the angry person often tries (consciously or unconsciously) to extract penance or retribution from the source of provocation. In both instances, the angry person's responses reflect the desire (conscious or unconscious) to punish the guilty party because anger and guilt are bedfellows.

Resentment is the result of anger that builds up over a period of time. Anger and resentment about uncertainty arise from the belief that one's needs should be met in a predictable and prompt way. People who need certainty, and who experience a lot of anxiety when facing uncertainty, tend to become angry when their unconscious attempts to cope with their anxiety lead them to blame someone or something for their discomfort. Although low tolerance for uncertainty may be the root cause, the need to ascribe blame is the immediate cause of their anger.

A New Way to Think About Anger and Resentment

The basis of the continued expression of anger and resentment is the tendency to lay blame, and to condemn or damn people and things. Therefore, as discussed below, the key to managing anger and resentment is to reduce the tendency to lay blame, and to stop condemning or damning people and things.

Fundamentally, the expression of anger is a choice; your choice. When you choose the expression of anger as a habitual manner of response, you are really choosing to avoid taking responsibility for your emotional reactions and responses. So, chronically angry people often say things like, "She *made me* angry" or "He *made me* depressed." Learning to manage anger in a healthy and functional way involves training yourself to become conscious of your "anger triggers," and then to choose alternative responses.

Angry feelings, resentment, and rage are associated with increased levels of adrenaline in the bloodstream, rapid heart beat, and a significant increase in blood pressure. Blood pressure increases as a result of the constriction or tightening of the small blood vessels, which include the coronary arteries.

Doctors Redford and Virginia Williams (1993) described this phenomenon in their book *Anger Kills*. They describe a condition they call the "hostility syndrome." People with this condition feel a high degree of irritability, an urge to act aggressively toward others in what they perceive as self-defense, an increased urge to smoke and overeat, a craving for high sugar and high fat foods, as well as an increase in alcohol consumption.

This creates a vicious cycle causing a loss of impulse control, which results in a greater tendency to act out aggressive and hostile feelings in a verbal or physical manner. Dr. Matthew McKay and his colleagues (1989) addressed this issue of acting out one's angry feelings. They listed the common myths associated with anger. These are:

- Anger is biochemically determined and results from a biochemical imbalance.

- Anger and aggression are instinctual for humans.

- Frustration leads to aggression.

- It is healthy to vent your anger.

In their book, Dr. McKay and his colleagues demonstrate how these four assumptions are incorrect, and how reality exhibits the opposite of all four myths.

The false assumption that venting your anger will diminish its intensity and make you feel better is very prevalent. It is based on another false assumption, which is that there can be an overflow of anger, as in a closed hydraulic system, that needs to be released; and that if it isn't released, the system will explode. People frequently use this idea in their daily language. For example, you may hear people say, "I need to let off some steam," or someone might give this advice to an angry friend, "You should go to the gym and punch the punching bag to get rid of your anger."

The fact is that these methods are not healthy for reducing angry feelings. First, human beings are not closed hydraulic systems; the analogy of releasing steam is not appropriate and does not apply to human behavior or to the constellation of emotions in the human mind. Second, these methods make the situation worse because feelings of anger that are acted out physically tend to transform into violent behavior. Third, studies show that the repeated experience of anger, aggression, and hostility, and the rapid discharge of these emotions, are associated with an increased risk of heart disease (Williams and Williams 1993).

Inappropriate management of your angry feelings also levies a high cost on your interpersonal relationships. It creates more conflicts at work with your superiors, peers, and subordinates. It creates disruptions and conflicts with members of your family and your friends. People who chronically mismanage their angry feelings become alienated from others, themselves, and the world. They also feel misunderstood and frequently blame others for their own behavior. This can lead to depression and more anger.

McKay and his colleagues (1989) assert that anger has a number of specific functions:

- The expression of anger can serve the immediate need to release tension. Having to tolerate uncertainty requires *frustration tolerance*. That means one has to be able to tolerate *delays of gratification*, or the possibility that one's needs may not be gratified at all.

- The experience and expression of anger can block out of awareness painful emotions such as anxiety, hurt, guilt, and so on. All of these painful emotions, as already discussed, may result from chronic uncertainty.

- The experience and expression of anger may cover up and dissipate underlying physical sensations of pain and discomfort. That is, the immediate momentary release of tension, which the expression of anger affords, may serve to block one's pain because the conscious mind can pay attention only to a limited number of things at one time. In this case, anger can be thought of as a distraction.

• The expression of anger also may serve to discharge stress associated with frustrated and unmet needs. For many people, understandably, not knowing if their needs are going to be met is frustrating.

• The expression of anger also may serve as a form of self-defense against a real or perceived threat. For many people, understandably, uncertainty is perceived as loaded with potential or actual threat.

Although the *expression* of anger may serve a number of important functions, it is usually not a functional response; in fact, it is usually dysfunctional. A functional response is one that leads to achieving your short-term and long-term goals for pleasure, the avoidance of pain, and the ability to lead a life that you define as fulfilling. Functionality leads to harmony on two levels; first, within you, harmony between mind and body, and second, harmony with other people. The excessive expression of anger creates disharmony or discord on both levels and frustrates the realization of your short-term and long-term goals.

Forgiveness

Frequently, anger originates with a need to find the responsible or guilty party, and then it leads to blaming that party as the cause of your anger. Anger also may lead to blaming yourself. Self-blame is associated with feelings of guilt and shame. One important way to relieve such negative feelings is to activate the power of forgiveness. That is your capacity to forgive yourself and others.

The act of forgiveness is erroneously associated in many people's minds with condoning unacceptable behavior. The truth is that forgiveness is truly a new way of thinking, feeling, and behaving *within yourself*. That is because it addresses *your* perceptions, thoughts, and feelings about the specific events and people that led to your anger and resentment.

For example, if someone acted in a way that hurt or humiliated you, your first reaction, understandably, might be to lash back at that person and extract a punishment, or to develop anger and resentment that might fester within you for some time. Ultimately, you have to decide what to do about your anger and resentment. If you continue to hold on to it, you will end up hurting yourself and poisoning your own body. So, you would be better off to find a way to let go of the poison.

Forgiveness is all about letting go of poisonous thoughts and feelings. It actually is a gift that you give to yourself for your own peace of mind and mind-body health. It is a form of cleansing your mind and your body. Honestly done, it heals your spirit and cleanses your soul. Forgiving the people who have offended you is not done for them, but for yourself.

For example, if you keep lashing back at someone who offended you as a way to continue to hurt or humiliate that person, you keep stoking the fires of anger and resentment in your own mind, body, and soul. This hurts you more than it hurts that person. One alternative could be to acknowledge that you have been offended or wronged, and then change your angry state of mind. If you have committed wrongs by your retaliatory actions, it might be in your own best interests to forgive yourself for your own actions.

Practical Solutions

The key to managing anger and resentment is to reduce the tendency to lay blame, condemn, or damn people and things. It is essential to accept that the expression of anger, in any circumstance, is your choice. It is also essential to become aware of when, where, and how your anger response is triggered, or what it is that trips your "anger switch."

There are times when anger is a spontaneous and reflexive response to a real or perceived threat to your personal safety, your reputation, or your self-esteem. When that happens, your response is likely to be sudden, quick, and experienced by you not as a choice but as a self-defense reflex. This reflex originates in your old mammalian brain called the limbic system. The limbic system is the seat of many emotions and has been referred to as the "emotional brain." It provides the quick recognition of threatening, dangerous situations, and it has an internal alarm system that warns you of danger by the sudden secretion of the neurotransmitter norepinephrine.

The best way to handle the limbic system's angry responses is to first respect them as designed to protect you from attack. However, what was a helpful and adaptive response becomes maladaptive when we habitually misperceive other people's behaviors as threats, and when the intensity of our response is inappropriate to the situation.

Our human brains are equipped with the latest evolutionary development called the *neocortex* or the *neo-mammalian* brain. This largest part of our brain is what is so unique to our species, *Homo sapiens.* It is what truly makes us human beings. The neocortex with its executive functions has the capacity to tame and reeducate our limbic-emotional brain.

In other words, by using the cognitive response of self-talk, we are able to establish and strengthen neuronal (nerve cell) communications with our limbic-emotional brain, and retrain its responses to make them more moderate and appropriate to specific situations. This involves the executive brain taking charge of our behavioral response by calming the intensity of our emotional experience and blocking its verbal or physical expression until it is processed by the executive brain.

One other function of anger when expressed on an interpersonal level is the delivery of a warning message such as, "Be careful, stop this behavior and get away from me," or "Do what I want you to do now!" The result in many cases is that the angry person pushes others away, or intimidates them into submission. However, what typically happens is that people who experience chronic angry responses that they express inappropriately, wind up feeling isolated, alienated, disconnected, and without true, close friends. People tend to become afraid of them and literally stay away from close encounters that are within the "danger zone."

Kevin's Story

Kevin is a thirty-three-year-old married father of three. He has had problems with managing his anger all of his life. His wife complains that he frequently lashes out at her and the children with strong words and threatening gestures. Although she perceives his behaviors as too extreme and inappropriate to whatever the situation at hand is, he believes that his responses are provoked by his wife's behavior, or that of his kids. Only hours and sometimes days later does he realize that his responses were indeed too intense and way out of proportion to the situation.

What Kevin sees initially as provocation, he is apt to see later on as rather trivial and unworthy of such strong, angry responses. He feels remorse and asks his wife and children to forgive him. His attempts to control these immediate, impulsive responses, however, have not been particularly successful.

In therapy sessions, he learned to identify an internal signal that in his particular case was physical in nature. It involved a sudden hot sensation in his face and throat. Knowing that this was a signal from his body that he was feeling angry and about to explode, he learned to put his hands together in a clasped position, take a deep breath, and physically remove himself from the situation that had triggered his anger. He was taught to go to another room in his home where he practices a calming relaxation exercise. At times, he listens to calming music, says a prayer, and gets himself centered by activating his executive brain to engage in cognitive self-talk.

At other times he has to begin the process by writing his thoughts in his journal. His self-talk might go like this:

Come on, Kevin. Just calm down. Just calm down. That's right, calm down. Remember me? I'm your inner friend. I'm the "voice of reason." You know me. You've heard me before. I truly want to protect you and I have your best interests in mind. I know you feel hurt and angry right now. However, we can process this together with a cool head and a calm heart. I know how much you love your wife and your children, and you know how much they love you, too. What just happened between you and your wife was a simple misunderstanding. This can be easily straightened out.

She did not know that you had already bought the gift for your cousin's anniversary, and she went ahead and bought the same gift herself. You forgot to tell her that you would do it. Her buying the gift was not meant to disrespect you. She wanted to help you and spare you the burden and the time of shopping for it. Both of you ended up spending money on the same gift. This can be easily resolved. One of you can return the gift and get a refund. Now, is this worth getting so angry about? Misunderstandings happen in all healthy families. All you need to do, when you are calm enough, is talk to your wife and together you can find the solution to this issue. Now doesn't that make good sense? Don't you feel better already? I can see the smile starting up on your face, knowing that you are beginning to feel better.

When Kevin is calm enough, he returns to the dialogue with his wife, and they resolve the problem in a rational way. He feels proud of himself that he did not allow his anger to explode.

This example demonstrates a specific technique called *adaptive disengagement*. Kevin physically disengaged from the interaction with his wife when his angry emotions became too intense. By doing so, he prevented his limbic-emotional brain from "hijacking" the rest of his brain into a rash, inappropriate, angry, emotional response. Practicing this exercise on a regular basis has helped Kevin to master his tendency to blow up in anger whenever he feels hurt or threatened. This experience of mastery also is self-empowering and is associated with increased self-esteem, as well as with improved relationships with his wife and children, and with his coworkers and friends.

Exercising the Solution

Forgiveness is a tool that can be used every day on an ongoing basis whenever your anger reflex is triggered and threatens to poison your experience and interfere with your ability to resolve a problem peacefully. It is easy to use this tool. All that's required is for you to *want* to control your anger and to *expect* to be able to do so. Here's how to use the forgiveness tool.

Whenever you feel angry, identify what or with whom you are angry. Do this as soon as you become aware that you are angry. Then, ask yourself exactly what has happened or exactly what that person has done that fired you up. Were the person's actions intended to hurt you? If it was a situation, was that situation designed specifically to hurt you?

It is easier to use the forgiveness tool if the answer to the two questions above is *No*. However, to strengthen your developing forgiveness skill, and to make your use of the forgiveness tool more powerful, assume the worst for the moment; that the affront was intentional and intended to hurt you.

When you pick up and use the forgiveness tool, you must first give yourself the chance to experience your anger as a signal that there has been an affront (so that you can take appropriate action to protect your personal safety and defend yourself, as well as those you love, if it is that type of situation). But you also must give yourself the chance to act responsibly with a cool as opposed to a hot head. You do this by giving yourself the benefit of letting go of the poison of anger so that you can respond with a clear head. So, say to yourself:

For me, but more so for my body, letting anger stay fired up is a poison. I need my body to live. Therefore, I owe my body the protection and respect that it deserves. That means keeping poison away from and out of my body. To the degree to which I want to protect and respect my body, I avoid letting myself get fired up with anger. This benefits my body, my heart, my soul, and my spirit.

When you make this commitment to your body and your health, by repeating this mantra on an ongoing basis, the basic idea becomes imprinted in your unconscious mind. The positive result is that the anger reflex or habit is weakened, and it becomes easier and easier to employ the forgiveness tool.

The other part of applying the forgiveness tool is to practice it regularly. The more you practice using it, the stronger it becomes. Using it is as simple as saying the following simple phrase to yourself whenever you get angry:

I forgive you [name of whoever or whatever offended you]. *I choose to give up my anger at you so that I can be free. I do this for myself and for those I love.*
Also, tell yourself the following:

I also forgive you [your own name]. *You* [your own name] *are human. You are a human being, and as a human, you are imperfect. I accept this.*
Practicing this exercise repeatedly makes it a practical, usable skill that can make your life more peaceful and less angry. Start doing it and begin to notice the positive changes in

your experience. Forgiveness frees you from the whims of others and from unpredictable events. It allows you to cope with the uncertainty as well as the predictability of others' cruel, insensitive, or just plain unacceptable behaviors, without damning yourself in the process.

Remember you are forgiving *for the benefit of yourself and for those you love*, not for the benefit of those you detest.

Another Solution. Identify and record in your journal your personal physical, mental, and emotional early signals that you are experiencing anger. Once you've identified those signals, test your observations in your daily life to confirm that your recognition of these signals is accurate.

Practicing the following centering exercise will prevent you from delivering inappropriate, threatening, and intimidating gestures. You will, instead, experience both of your hands coming together in a clasped position.

Do this exercise in the privacy of your own room. Sit in a chair, take a deep breath, slowly exhale, and as you exhale, squeeze your hands together in a clasped position. This special *centering* exercise prevents your hands and arms from delivering angry gestures of any kind. It symbolically communicates the sense of coming together; the form of your two hands hugging each other and centering in order to activate your rational, executive brain to take action. Now, take another deep breath to calm down even more, and listen to your rational brain as it guides you through this calming exercise, and introduces a new way to process the interaction that triggered your angry feelings.

Clasping your hands together also represents the cooperation between the two parts of your mind, your conscious and unconscious. When both parts of your mind cooperate instead of fighting each other, you will feel less conflict and stress.

Make it a habit to practice this exercise on a daily basis and write down what were the issues or the situation that triggered your angry response in your journal (or on a piece of paper when the journal is not with you). Do this as close in time to the experience of your anger as is possible. This will allow a more mature expression of your feelings. Using written words indirectly activates your more mature, rational brain. However, you must be careful not to use foul language for the healthy expression of your feelings. The use of curse words, even when written in your personal journal, perpetuates inappropriate blaming, damning, and demonizing of other people and situations, and blocks the progress of your mastery over your anger.

You must also remember that your progress will not take place in a straight line. Instead, you may, at times, take one step backwards after you have taken three steps forward. This is natural and to be expected. It does not indicate failure, so avoid calling it a *relapse*, because it is not. Accept this as part of your natural growth progression, and learn to forgive yourself for not being perfect. Practice forgiving yourself as you proceed with this discipline. When you conscientiously continue to do this, you will find that you will also begin to forgive yourself for the mistakes you made in the past. This will raise your self-esteem. Additionally, it will help you to realize that forgiving someone is not a sign of weakness, but a sign of strength.

Connect with Others
and Create Meaning

I will act as if what I do makes a difference.

—William James

Connect with others and create meaning because a meaningless life is barren and empty. There are times when faced with chronic uncertainty and our inability to change or control it, that we experience a sense of futility, or nihilism, and we may believe that life is worthless and without meaning. Typically, this happens following disasters when innocent people die without any just cause or reason, and we have a hard time making sense of why it happened. We also can't make sense of why some people survive and others perish. These are the times when we feel alone, let down, and alienated from the world and perhaps also from God.

These feelings originate from the belief that every event in our world has a purpose. They also originate from a belief system that views God as all-knowing and all-powerful. This view naturally invites the question of where is God when horrible disasters natural or man-made happen. Here are some typical questions that follow from this point of view:

- Why did God not prevent this?

- If God is all-just, all-knowing, and all-powerful, does that mean that the people who died were not really innocent, and that they deserved to die? Does that mean the disaster was a manifestation of God's wrath and anger, punishing the sinners and extinguishing evil?

- We know that innocent people do die, and if we continue to accept God as just and filled with wisdom, how do we then make sense of what happened?

Some people deal with this dilemma by adopting the sarcastic, nihilistic position that states, "Life is a bitch and then you die." However, this position only reinforces the individual's sense of confusion, alienation, and despair.

A New Way to Think About the Problem

The question of why God allows a particular atrocity or catastrophe to happen actually dates back to ancient civilizations. Some say that the Book of Job in the Bible is devoted to examining just this question. A more recent book by Rabbi Harold Kushner (1981) addresses the question for our modern era with the proposition that perhaps we must revise our concept of God, whereby God should not be viewed as all-powerful. Rather, it might be helpful to think of God as needing us to be his partners in completing the act of creation, by fighting evil and strengthening goodness and kindness in the world.

This is not a new position. It was also expressed by the prominent American philosopher-physician, Dr. William James, at the turn of the nineteenth century (1984). He advocated the belief that God created the world, but left creation incomplete.

The world has a good deal of evil in it. God needs our help in eradicating evil and supporting virtue. Human beings should make it their mission in life to become God's partners in repairing and completing the world by combating evil and strengthening goodness.

It is important to think about your life and to live it as if everything you do has meaning. Even the smallest and most insignificant of actions potentially can have consequences that extend far beyond the immediate present. Ironically, when you stay centered in the present and treat whatever you do as *your* actions emanating from *your* choices, you empower yourself, and at the same time, you respect others. This is because when you hold this attitude, you accept total responsibility for *your* actions and choices.

Practical Solutions

How do we implement solutions in daily life that will serve as antidotes to alienation, disconnection, and nihilism? Part of the answer can be found in the attitude and philosophy described in the paragraph above. When you accept total responsibility for *your* actions and *your* choices, you begin to value every action and every choice that you make. You begin to think and feel that everything you do is important and matters, and that in fact, you are important. This is a very powerful antidote to alienation.

You become more aware of the distinction between *yourself* as person, and *others* as people too; they are separate from you, but yet affected by what you do. This view leads you to think of the world as an interrelated whole. This means that every thought and action count. Many philosophers and world leaders believe that we humans will do better if we see ourselves as part of a larger whole. The feeling of being connected to a Higher Power may contribute to a sense of connectedness, making us feel part of a larger community.

According to Martin Buber (1974), viewing another as an "it" is a selfish, self-centered, and narcissistic position that is a remnant from childhood. This immature position views other people as *things* or tools to be used, exploited, and dispensed with when they are no longer needed. According to this narcissistic view, others' feelings, wishes, and needs are irrelevant to *our* needs.

The real turning point in transforming into a mature spiritual adult from an immature child is the recognition that another person is not an "it," but rather a "thou." What that means is the recognition and acceptance of the fact that other people are just as human as we are, and that they, too, have the right to live in this world and enjoy the gifts of nature and the social community.

Viewing another as a "thou" indicates our recognition that other people have feelings, wishes, desires, and dreams just as we do, and have the right to be treated with the same respect and dignity as we do. This view helps us accept the common humanity we share with others' even when they belong to different races, cultures, nationalities, or religions, or when they espouse different philosophies, opinions, or belief systems.

In *God in Search of Man* (1956), Rabbi Abraham J. Heschel also presents the idea that God needs us to be his partners in completing the act of creation. For him, this idea translates to the need to perform acts of kindness and charity in caring for our fellow human beings. Engaging in such activities, which Jewish people call *mitzvot*, reaffirms our sense of the covenant we have with our Higher Power, and consolidates our feelings of connectedness and the sense of purpose we have in our lives. We begin to feel that we are here for a purpose; that our lives have meaning.

The issue of having a life filled with meaning is of vital importance. For example, Dr. Viktor Frankl (1959), the Jewish-Austrian psychiatrist who survived horrific ordeals in the German concentration camps of World War II, described how having a meaningful life filled with purpose helped him to endure the horrors of the Nazi death camps; and prevented him from giving up in the face of terrible adversity, torture, and hopelessness.

Doctors who are spiritual in their philosophy of life and in their practice of medicine recognize their patients' need for a meaning to their symptoms, and they address this need in their medical work (Dossey 1991). This translates into treating the patient as a whole person rather than being focused solely on the treatment of the disease. Such a spiritual-medical philosophy was summarized by the famous physician and professor of medicine, Sir William Osler, when he said, "It is more important to know what kind of patient has a disease than the kind of disease the patient has" (Bliss 1999).

Exercising the Solution

The following are meditative, imagery exercises designed to help you get in touch with your higher spiritual self:

Torem's Back from the Future Technique (Torem 1992)

Put yourself in a comfortable position sitting or reclining in your favorite chair at home or in your safe place. Eliminate all distractions. Put your hands in a clasped position. Feel your two hands as they come together with the fingers intertwined touching each other and squeezing gently as if hugging each other with recognition of coming together for an important meeting. Take a deep breath, and as you slowly exhale, let your eyelids close and your body float. You can use any favorite image of floating that you are comfortable with.

As you continue to breathe comfortably at your own pace and rhythm, experience your feet touching the floor or resting on a footrest. You are, in fact, on a solid foundation, well-grounded and safe. Experience the air coming into your chest and expanding into your lungs with fresh, abundant oxygen.

Open a new channel of concentration whereby you experience yourself in a special time machine. You are now able to fly into the future. Set a time of one, two, or three years from the present. Let the time machine land in a place of your desire; ideally a place of your positive dreams. It has a superb climate and ideal weather. You are with people who treat you with respect and dignity. You feel a strong sense of inner peace and comfort. The surroundings affirm and validate your positive internal feelings.

You are able to recognize the beauty in the world around you. You see this beauty in nature; in the trees, the flowers, the shrubs, the animals, the sky, the rivers and creeks, the lakes and ponds, and in all the living creatures. You see yourself as a connected part of this majestic beauty. You are part of the universe and an integral example of God's creation. There is a purpose for you having been born, for you being alive, and for you to go on living. You now live with a sense of purpose.

You engage daily in acts of kindness to other living beings. These experiences enhance your sense of well-being and your image of yourself as a kind, charitable, and positive caring person. You feel you have become a true partner with your Higher Power, having entered into a sacred covenant which involves making a commitment to do good by every action you take, and to repair the world when it suffers from acts of evil.

Now absorb all of these experiences, feelings, and sensations on both conscious and unconscious levels, and bring them back with you as special gifts, as you come traveling back from the future into the present in your time machine. When you land in the present and emerge from your imaginary time machine, notice what a wonderful sense of peace and serenity you now experience.

Let these special feelings stay with you and guide you every day whether you are awake or asleep, whether you are consciously aware or tuned out. Let this be your experience every day of the week, every week of the month, and every month of the year, as you move forward on your special journey of connecting and reconnecting with your Higher Power as you affirm your faith and belief that life is worth living, meaningful, and that you have a purpose in it.

Now go ahead and take a deep breath and get ready to shift gears to the reality of the present. As you exhale, allow your eyelids to slowly open. Notice how your eyes come back into focus. You are becoming fully awake, alert, and completely oriented to your surroundings. Now you are ready to assume your adaptive functioning in your activities of day-to-day living.

Now consider this second exercise:

Focusing Exercise

Situate yourself comfortably in an upright chair with your back well supported and your feet flat on the floor. Place your hands on your lap and close your eyes. Keep your eyes closed comfortably and gently. Do not squeeze them tight. If your eyelids begin to flutter, this is normal, and soon you won't pay attention to it.

Now, concentrate on your breathing without trying to change it. Just let yourself breathe easily, comfortably, and normally. Soon you find that your breathing changes by itself; it becomes slower, more even and regular, and more rhythmic. If your mind should wander, the moment you realize it has wandered, gently bring your attention back to your breathing. Soon, you find yourself feeling much more relaxed and calm. You feel even more serene and relaxed with every breath, inhaling relaxation and exhaling tensions and stress.

When you are ready, and you feel noticeably more relaxed, a special word or short simple phrase comes to your mind. This word or short phrase is associated with the feelings of peace, love, connectedness, gratitude, appreciation, and contentment. Enjoy the present moment. It is sacred and special. You are alive and you are experiencing the wonderful gift of living. As you continue to breathe in and out, you listen to the sound of the special word or short phrase that your unconscious mind has brought to the center of your attention.

While you continue to focus your attention on this word or phrase and on your breathing, you experience the special light of life that is ever-present and never extinguished. When you know that you remain comfortable in the here and now of the present moment, and you continue to feel the strength connecting you with your positive future, you are now ready to open your eyes and return to alert and awake focus.

Make It a Habit to Perform Acts of Kindness

It is well-established in the wisdom of many cultures that reality is defined by actions. It is the *act* that counts, much more than the *thought*. The activities that you engage in every day, in your ordinary life, define your reality. They clearly show what you value by demonstrating where you put your time and energy.

Acts of kindness empower and solidify your identity as a good person, and indirectly enhance your positive self-esteem. The Jewish physician-philosopher, Rabbi Moses Maimonides, wrote that good deeds and acts of kindness and compassion not only support and help the one receiving the kindness, but help the one giving the kindness even more (1975).

Abigail Van Buren, who wrote the syndicated "Dear Abby" column for many years, once said that the best index of a person's *true* character was how he treated people who couldn't do him any harm or good, and how he treated people who could not fight back or hurt him. She was referring to pure acts of kindness unmotivated by any reasons of self-interest.

Remember that every day is a new day. You are the master of what you do and how you conduct yourself today. Each new day offers you many opportunities to act in a caring way and to perform acts of kindnesses for others. Besides taking care of your routine activities and rituals today, engage in actions that give the world more kindness and goodness. Remember John Lennon's proclamation that *"in the end the love you take is equal to the love you make."*

As examples of acts of pure kindness, consider the following list:

- Consider volunteering at a place of selfless service, such as at a hospital, nursing home, hospice, or homeless shelter.

- Eliminate swear words from your language. Such words demean the value of yourself and others and fuel needless anger.

- Consider being polite on the road to other drivers.

- Consider embracing your uncertainties today as a gift that allows you to discover goodness, and to experience pleasant surprise and heartfelt satisfaction when goodness does happen.

- Consider how you can feel grateful for the goodness that sustains you today and makes your life more comfortable. Also, consider how you can express gratitude in deeds of kindness that make you and others feel better and more appreciative.

- Consider what you can do today that will be solely for the benefit of somebody else (the "thou" that Buber wrote about).

- "If you do a good job for others, you heal yourself at the same time, because a dose of joy is a spiritual cure. It transcends all barriers." (Ed Sullivan)

Define Your Purpose and Meaning in Life

It is vitally important that you have a personal credo, faith, philosophy, or belief system. It will help you to clarify what your credo is if you write it down. For example, you may say; my personal credo is to be a loyal friend and partner to my spouse; a loving, responsible parent to my children; and to establish meaningful connections with my friends and fellow human beings. I see myself as striving for higher levels of personal integrity and credibility, being connected with my Higher Power, and seeing God in the daily wonders of life and nature.

Now, sit down and write out your own personal credo which connects the different aspects of your belief system in a positive way. This credo of your organized belief system should include your sense of mission in life as well as your vision for the future.

In phase two of this exercise, write down actions and behaviors that are compatible with your personal credo, and list separately those actions that can move you closer to your positive vision. This activity can be revised and modified on a regular basis, especially following personally meaningful experiences, such as reading a book, watching a movie, or interacting with other people. This list may also include getting through painful events in your life such as the loss of a loved one, or the experience of grief. You may also include other milestones such as job promotions, school graduations, getting married, the birth of a child or grandchild, and so on.

Activating Your Center Core

The following exercise adapted from Torem and Gainer (1995) will help you to get in touch with that unique aspect of yourself that is identified as the *positive, healthy you*. This is the inner part of yourself that makes you unique and special. It has been with you over your entire lifetime and has helped you to survive and thrive through difficult predicaments in the face of uncertainty.

Take several deep relaxing breaths and read these words very slowly, a few words at a time. After you've taken several deep relaxing breaths, let your breathing return to normal and to settle into a nice, even, calm, comfortable, relaxing rhythm. Now consider the following:

Deep within you there is a center core that is intelligent, wise, creative, logical, protective, relaxed, and confident. It wants you to heal and be well. It knows that you can cope with uncertainty and it helps you to do so. It is dedicated to your well-being and to helping you make meaning out of the unknown, as well as out of the known—what you have done and experienced in the past. This part of you knows much more than you consciously know or think you know.

This inner core can be thought of as your inner advisor or internal guide. Some refer to it as a "guardian angel" or "spirit guide" from within. Regardless of what you call it, it is part of you. And it has the very special and important functions of guiding you from within and helping you to make the best choices in your life.

Now, imagine and experience yourself in a peaceful and safe place feeling prepared to meet this center core part of yourself. When it makes its presence known, thank it for coming forward. Ask it how it would like to be addressed. Ask it if it's all right with it for you to ask any questions that come to your mind that you would like to have answered now. [Most likely your inner advisor will oblige.]

This is the time to ask your inner advisor how you can best think, feel, and act to cope with any difficult or uncertain situation you may be in now. Wait for an answer to come to mind in the form of words, images, sensations, or memories. As you become aware of these responses, reflect on them, and feel free to ask your inner advisor for further clarification at any time.

Realize that your inner advisor is an important source of inner strength and knowledge who is always with you. It helps you find your path in life. By developing the habit and the skills of consulting with it, you empower yourself. You develop your ability to tap into your own inner intelligence and wisdom. This helps you make choices in the present by connecting you to experiences from the past that provide lessons you can use in the present and in the future (Torem 1997).

When you are ready to end this exercise and emerge from your self-relaxation, do so by counting out loud from one to five. At the count of five, you feel alert, awake, renewed, and refreshed, with a stronger and renewed sense of purpose and confidence, and at the same time, feeling much more relaxed and comfortable.

In the Talmud, which is a written record of the dialogues and disputations of scholars and rabbis about Jewish law as written in the Torah (the Five Books of Moses), Rabbi Hillel once stated his version of the Golden Rule: *What is hateful to you, don't do to others.* When more people in the world follow this rule, the world will be a much more peaceful place. Although you have no direct control over how others behave, your own behavior does make a difference. You too can follow the Golden Rule, and consider practicing the words of the Prophet Micah; "What the Lord requires of you, only to do justice and to love goodness and to walk humbly with your God" (Micah, 6:8).

Learn to Be Flexible

All we have to do in life is to decide what to do with the time we have.

—J. R. R. Tolkien,
The Lord of the Rings

Learn to be flexible so you don't break. Flexibility is the way to survive uncertainty. It is a disadvantage to be rigid. The willow tree that flexes survives the strongest gale, but the tall, rigid tree that resists is eventually felled by strong winds. So, what appears to be strong and solid on the outside actually can have detrimental internal features when standing up to the forces of nature.

Nothing in this life is for certain. We have to live our lives knowing that we cannot know for sure what will happen tomorrow. We can make our plans and conduct our daily routines, but in the end, we can never know what tomorrow will bring. Flexibility means being capable of continually adapting and adjusting to a changing world.

Societies and human beings that are able to adapt and change are the ones that survive. So, being flexible is advantageous to surviving and thriving in the face of all the change all around us. Being rigid is disadvantageous because it often leads to maladaptive and ineffective coping, and may even lead to demise.

Rigidity is actually a form of denial. This means that it is associated with refusing to acknowledge reality—whether it is a disaster, a loss, or a change in our own bodies, such as changes brought about by aging or disease. Being flexible is equivalent to acceptance of the facts of reality. It means acknowledging that the change has occurred, and doing what you can to adjust to that change, for your own sake, and for the sake of your loved ones.

Rigidity is associated with stagnation and being stuck. What you resist dealing with tends to persist. Even worse, rigidly denying the existence of a problem that needs to be addressed can create a greater problem later on. So, rigidity can be viewed as a form of denial in the face of change. It is holding on to a specific point of view regardless of what has happened around you. It is ignoring reality and escaping into fantasy.

This form of coping causes trouble not only for you but also for the people around you. Refusing to accept reality does not change reality; rather, it exposes you to greater dangers, like the ostrich who sticks its head in the sand to avoid danger. Recognizing the approaching storm and finding proper shelter is by far the better coping strategy. Consider the following folk tale:

An old man was sitting in his house listening to the news on the radio. He heard a warning of a probable flood in his neighborhood resulting from torrential rains and the nearby river rising above its banks. Shortly after he heard the news, water began to flood his basement. Then, the water rose and began to flood his first floor. So, the old man ran up to the second floor to seek protection. The waters rose to the second floor. So, the old man went up to his attic and climbed up onto the roof. A boat passed by, and the man's neighbor asked him to get in the boat to save his life. The old man refused to leave his house and replied, "I have faith in my Lord. God will protect me and save me." As the water kept rising, a police boat passed by and wanted to pick up the old man. But he refused the offer of help again, saying that his God would protect him and not allow him to drown.

Finally, a police rescue helicopter flew above the man's house and threw down a ladder. Still the old man refused to leave his perch stating that he still had faith that God would protect him. Finally the waters were so high, the raging river took down the whole house, and the old man drowned.

Then his soul came before God. The old man said to God, "My dear Lord, I was always your loyal servant. I followed all of your laws and rituals of practice. Why did you forsake me and allow me to drown?" God replied, "My dear man, I sent you a neighbor, and you refused to get on his boat. Then I sent you a police rescue boat, and still you refused help. And when I sent you the police rescue helicopter and threw you down a ladder, you still rigidly refused! What else could I have done in the face of your rigid refusals?"

Our daily rituals provide us with some measure of predictability and certainty. They organize our lives and make our day-to-day living comfortable. However, there come times in our lives when events take place that either we have not counted on happening, or that we have dreaded happening all of our lives. Here, we are speaking about the loss of loved ones, and unexpected accidents or disasters, natural or of human origin.

Life itself continually brings changes. Just as day turns into night and the seasons change, the years march on, and the world changes. Some changes are brought about by natural forces, such as the seasons or the weather. Other changes are man-made involving technological, economic, and political change. Some of these human-initiated changes occur quite quickly over relatively short periods of time; for example, corporate takeovers and buyouts, mass downsizing of companies, massive company bankruptcies, as well as political leadership and legislative or law-making changes.

Other man-made changes fall into the class of criminal acts or acts of terrorism that wreak havoc in the daily life of civilized societies. It is normal to ask ourselves after surviving such an event, "How could such a thing happen?" It is also normal to cope with the first phase of shock and disbelief by partial denial. Everyone also searches for explanations of why it happened, and everyone develops all sorts of theories to make sense of the senseless and the unthinkable.

However, it is only those societies and people who are willing to accept the reality of what happened, and who keep their minds open and flexible, that will arrive at the necessary, creative solutions to handle such horrific events effectively. In other words, being flexible not only requires acceptance of reality, but it also sets the stage that is necessary for creative, intelligent solution-making.

Exercising Flexibility

Flexibility means changing your plans and your actions in the face of new unexpected developments. It means reassessing your priorities and coping strategies continually, as you are faced with the new demands of reality. It requires you to be able to shift gears one to the other, and to exercise good judgment regarding your priorities.

Life continually brings in new variables that require flexibility in finding the most adaptive and creative solutions. If you are solution-oriented, you must be continually prepared to change your priorities based on the demands of reality. To be flexible, you have to have a strong foundation of good judgment, so you can adjust your priorities appropriately, when necessary.

The following example illustrates the benefits of being flexible. When you stretch the muscles of your body regularly and do not overdo it, you increase your range of motion. Similarly, when you stretch your mind, you increase your range of responses. Consider the following scenario:

Joan was working on a presentation on marketing strategies regarding the launching of a new product, and she had a deadline to meet. On Monday morning at ten A.M., she was scheduled to present her plan to her boss. As she worked out the fine details of her presentation, she received a phone call from Florida informing her that her mother had just been admitted to an intensive care unit after sustaining a massive heart attack. She heard her father's anxious, trembling voice asking her to help him with a decision regarding her mother's treatment. She was now faced with a dilemma.

She would have to drop everything to fly down to Florida to be with her parents to support her father in his decisions regarding her mother's care. On the other hand, she could

continue with her original plan to finish her project and present it on Monday morning.

To successfully handle this dilemma, Joan had to abandon rigidity and embrace flexibility. She had to accept the reality that the new unexpected development of her mother's sudden illness was forcing her to make an important choice. On one hand, she might have ignored her parents' emergency and rigidly continued to address her own career plans. On the other hand, she might have shifted gears and examined her priorities. She recognized that this new reality required her to be flexible and to change her original plans.

Having a solid grasp of the important priorities in her life, she knew what took precedence. So, Joan changed her plans, shifted gears, postponed her presentation, and made reservations for the earliest flight to Florida.

In the same way that Joan did, staying flexible means reassessing your reality, examining your response options, and creatively planning the best approach, always taking into account any new developments.

Here is another example of solution-oriented thinking in action. Consider the following scenario:

You need to go to your doctor's office tomorrow to keep an appointment to check out a symptom that you have been concerned about for three months. That evening, your spouse or significant other calls you on the way home from work to tell you that his or her car has broken down. So, you pick your spouse up and the car is towed to the auto repair shop. Now you have to drive your spouse to work tomorrow, and you will be unable to get to your doctor's appointment on time. What do you do?

Well, the next morning, while you are driving your spouse to work, you call the doctor's office to explain the situation and ask if you can come in an hour later. The receptionist tells you that this is impossible because the doctor has to leave the office early. She informs you that you are going to have to reschedule. The next available appointment is in another two months; she cannot schedule you any sooner. So how do you handle this?

You handle this disappointment by asking politely if there is any way that you can be scheduled sooner. The response is "No way." Being rigid may lead you to lash out at the receptionist for being so insensitive to your needs, and for being so rigid. However, lashing out at the receptionist is unlikely to get you what you want. A better alternative would be to shift gears mentally and emotionally, and accept the fact that you have chosen to drive your spouse, to work rather than keep your doctor's appointment. This was your choice, and with it came the consequences of a new reality; that is, having to postpone the appointment with your doctor.

With this more flexible attitude, you politely thank the receptionist for giving you the next available appointment and for agreeing to put you on the call list if there are any cancellations. Although you are disappointed that you must continue to wait for an appointment with the doctor, you are pleased with yourself for having kept your cool, and for having stayed solution-oriented in your attitude and approach to the dilemma.

Remember, you cannot be in two places at the same time. Whining and complaining about this only amounts to denying this reality and delays you from making the right choice as to how you are going to respond to the unexpected. Obsessing about not being able to be in two places at once unnecessarily splits your attention and disrupts your smooth functioning. You know that the best choice in times like these is to choose a response based on your rational, cool-headed assessment of what has top priority, and then act accordingly. By doing so, you adjust to the unexpected and you feel good about yourself.

The syndicated newspaper columnist Ann Landers once said that *opportunities are usually disguised as hard work, so most people do not recognize them*. This observation points out that crises and problems often provide fertile grounds for finding new opportunities. However, the problems must be addressed and tackled. A crisis is really just a problem that smacks you so hard in the face that you cannot ignore it.

Flexibility in the face of change yields immeasurable opportunities for positive growth and renewal. Innovations and progress result from flexibility. When you work on improving your flexibility, you spark your creativity, and increase your opportunities for discovering answers to your problems that you might never have thought of had you not encountered your problems. This is why Norman Cousins in *Anatomy of an Illness* (1991) stated that "death is not the greatest loss in life. The greatest loss is what dies inside us while we live."

Cousins provided a very personal glimpse into what it's like to face the uncertainties created by a progressive, chronic illness on a daily basis. He explained how he coped with the uncertainties of his illness, and halted the progression of his symptoms by using positive thinking strategies and liberal helpings of humor.

Coping well with uncertainty of all kinds requires flexibility. Being flexible, that is, agile, adaptive, adjustable, easygoing, and functional, necessitates finding a functional balance between the two opposing forces of *acceptance* and *change*. Coping with uncertainty effectively requires an accommodation between these two opposing forces (Eimer 2002).

Constructive action and effective coping depend on acknowledging what is, even if you don't like it. If you can find a way to accept and understand your problems and adversities, you will find that it's easier to cope with them and you will be more functional and balanced in your daily living. Fear can paralyze you, and make the anxiety of not knowing what will happen worse. When you cultivate your ability to let go of paralyzing fear, you also develop a healthier relationship with yourself and uncertainty.

One of us previously wrote a book that focuses on using the tool of self-hypnosis to cope with chronic physical pain (Eimer 2002). In it, there is an outline, a "roadmap," for coping with change. It is labeled with the acronym, "A.W.A.R.E." This outline was constructed on these two basic ideas: (1) to be *aware* need not mean being obsessed or preoccupied with negatives (Zarren and Eimer 2001); and (2) healthy awareness is the necessary precondition to changing anything. You need to know (become aware of) what needs to be changed in order to develop a strategy for changing it. As the old adage puts it, *if you don't know where you're going, you're going to end up somewhere else.*

The acronym, A.W.A.R.E. stands for: Accept uncertainty as a given; Watch what you're experiencing (be a wise and participating observer); Act functionally despite your anxieties, fears, and discomforts; Remove yourself from unnecessary conflict and pain; and Expect the best.

Awareness and *acceptance* go hand in hand. You need not necessarily like a particular change or even change itself in general, but you do need to accept it and you need to accept yourself unconditionally to be in a position to take constructive, solution-oriented action. As stated above, *awareness* and *acceptance* do not mean *not* changing. On the contrary, rejecting and refusing to acknowledge and accept the reality of change may prevent you from initiating and continuing the process of genuine and healthy growth through adaptive personal change.

The psychologist Marsha Linehan (1993) wisely pointed out that the key to effective therapy for facilitating change with regard to chronic problems is learning how to balance *actively striving for change* and *inwardly searching for acceptance.*

Yes. You *can* do it. You have all the tools you need to continue improving how you cope with uncertainty *now*. We hope that you have found reading this book a valuable, enjoyable adventure, and a helpful and useful experience. We wish you the best as you implement the ideas, skills, and deeds into your activities of daily living. May you be blessed with courage in the face of uncertainty.

Summary

In this brief book, we have provided you with ten simple solutions for coping with uncertainty. These solutions can help you to cope more comfortably. By coping more comfortably we mean that you obsess less and worry less. You handle your frustrations and anxieties better, think more clearly, forgive yourself and others more easily, and form more humane connections with others.

In the Talmud, it is written that "Deeds of kindness are equal in weight to all the commandments." Perhaps that is what life is really all about—being kind. Small acts of kindness, as discussed in chapter 9, do as much for the *giver* as they do for the receiver. Even in the midst of the hell of the Nazi holocaust in World War II, the adolescent Anne Frank was able to write in her diary, "Think of all the beauty that's still left in and around you and be happy!" (1993). Surely, the doomed Anne Frank was a kind person!

The nineteenth-century philosopher, Ralph Waldo Emerson, said, "Make the most of yourself . . . for that is all there is of you." Perhaps that is the spirit by which we can achieve earthly "salvation" as we face the uncertainties that lie ahead. By performing acts of kindness for other people, you make the most of yourself and the world will be a better place for all of us.

You can cope much more comfortably with uncertainty by adopting the following ten simple solutions and making them a part of your life:

1. Accept uncertainty as part of life because *it is.*

2. Evaluate your real risks so you can prepare yourself to deal with *any* eventuality.

3. Change obsessive thoughts so you don't waste energy worrying.

4. Restore *inner* harmony so your mind and body function together as *one.*

5. Release tension so you can renew and replenish yourself.

6. Improve your tolerance for frustration so you can weather *any* storm.

7. Develop healthy self-acceptance because you owe it to *yourself.*

8. Learn to forgive yourself and others and set yourself free.

9. Connect with others and create meaning because a meaningless life is barren and empty.

10. Learn to be flexible so you don't break.

Do the exercises in the previous chapters and repeat these principles to yourself daily. These actions will imprint these key principles into your brain and they will become second nature. This means that they will become habits of thought, belief, feeling, and action. It is truly simple and also easy. This process will give you the edge you need to make uncertainty a welcome part of your perspective on life, and your life will be filled with more purpose and meaning.

References

Beck, A. T. 1976. *Cognitive Therapy and the Emotional Disorders*. New York: New American Library.

Bliss, M. 1999. *William Osler: A Life in Medicine*. London: Oxford University Press.

Buber, M. 1974. *I and Thou*. New York: Scribner's.

Cousins, N. 1991. *Anatomy of an Illness as Perceived by The Patient*. New York: Bantam Doubleday.

Dossey, L. 1991. *Meaning and Medicine*. New York: Bantam Books.

Eimer, B. N. 2002. *Hypnotize Yourself Out of Pain Now!* Oakland, CA: New Harbinger Publications.

Ellis, A. 1998. *How to Control Your Anxiety Before It Controls You*. Secaucus, NJ: Carol Publishing Group.

_____. 2001. *Overcoming Destructive Beliefs, Feelings, and Behaviors*. Amherst, NY: Prometheus Books.

Frank, A. 1993. *Anne Frank: The Diary of a Young Girl*. New York: Prentice Hall.

Frankl, V. E. 1959. *Man's Search for Meaning: An Introduction to Logotherapy*. Boston: Beacon Press.

Heschl, A. J. 1956. *God in Search of Man*. Philadelphia: Jewish Publications Society of America.

Horney, K. 1993. *Our Inner Conflicts: A Constructive Theory of Neurosis*. Reissued edition. New York: W.W. Norton.

James, W. 1997. *The Varieties of Religious Experience*. New York: Scribner's.

Johnson, K. Demanding a diagnosis, and outwitting anthrax. *The New York Times*, Dec. 3, 2001.

Kierkegaard, Soren. 2000. In *The Essential Kierkegaard*, edited by H. V. and E. H. Hong. Princeton, NJ: Princeton University Press.

Kushner, H. 1981. *When Bad Things Happen to Good People*. New York: Schocken Books.

Linehan, M. M. 1993. *Cognitive-Behavioral Treatment of Borderline Personality Disorder*. New York: Guilford.

Maimonides, M. 1975. *Essential Writings of Maimonides*. New York: New York University Press.

McCain, J., and M. Salter. 1999. *Faith of My Fathers*. New York: Random House.

McKay, M., P. Rogers, and J. McKay. 1989. *When Anger Hurts: Quieting the Storm Within*. Oakland, CA: New Harbinger Publications.

Rossi, E. L. 1991. *The 20 Minute Break: Using the New Science of Ultradian Rhythms*. New York: St. Martin's Press.

Schmidt, M. A. 2001. *Brain-Building Nutrition: The Healing Power of Fats and Oils*. Berkeley, CA: Frog, Ltd.

Schwartz, J. M. 1996. *Brain Lock: Free Yourself from Obsessive-Compulsive Behavior*. New York: HarperCollins.

Simonton, O. C., C. Simonton, S. Matthews, and J. L. Creighton. 1991. *Getting Well Again*. New York: Bantam Books.

Torem, M. S. 1992. Back from the future; A powerful age progression technique. *American Journal of Clinical Hynosis* 35:81–88.

————. 1998. Diagnostic and therapeutic uses of "inner-advisor" imagery. *Hypnos* 24:107–109.

Torem, M. S., and M. J. Gainer. 1995. The center-core; Imagery for experiencing the unifying self. *Hypnos* 22:125–131.

Watkins, J. G., and H. H. Watkins. 1997. *Ego States: Theory and Therapy.* New York: W. W. Norton.

Williams, R. B., and V. Williams. 1993. *Anger Kills: Seventeen Strategies for Controlling Hostility That Can Harm Your Health.* New York: Random House.

Zarren, J. I., and B. N. Eimer. 2001. *Brief Cognitive Hypnosis: Facilitating the Change of Dysfunctional Behavior.* New York: Springer Publishing Company.

Bruce N. Eimer, Ph.D., A.B.P.P., is a clinical psychologist with over fifteen years of experience treating people with cognitive-behavioral and self-help strategies. He currently works with patients dealing with anxiety, trauma, and chronic pain in private practice in Huntingdon, Pennsylvania. Eimer is a Board Diplomate of the American Board of Professional Psychology in the specialty of Behavioral Psychology, and holds board certifications in pain management, medical psychotherapy, and vocational neuropsychology. He is also certified by the American Society of Clinical Hypnosis as an Approved Consultant in Clinical Hypnosis. Eimer is a chronic pain survivor. He has also written *Hypnotize Yourself Out of Pain Now!*

Moshe S. Torem, M.D., is the Founder and Medical Director for the Center for Mind-Body Medicine at Akron's General Hospital Health and Wellness Center in Akron Ohio. He is also an Examiner on the American Board of Psychiatry and Neurology and was the Chairman of the Department of Psychiatry at Northeastern Ohio University. He has super-  vised or taught at several hospitals in Ohio and is a member of numerous societies including the American Society of Clinical Hypnosis, and Academy of Psychosomatic Medicine. He has written over 100 articles for professional journals, including *American Journal of Psychiatry*, *Contemporary Psychiatry*, *Psychiatry Law and Ethics*, and *Psychiatric Medicine*. Dr. Torem has also been the recipient of various awards, including the Distinguished Service Award from The General Assembly of the State of Ohio Senate and three Golden Apple Awards for Excellence in Teaching from Akron General Medical Center, Department of Psychiatry, and Northeastern Ohio Universities, College of Medicine, Department of Psychiatry.

Some Other New Harbinger Titles

The Stop Walking on Eggshells Workbook, Item SWEW $18.95

Conquer Your Critical Inner Voice, Item CYIC $15.95

The PTSD Workbook, Item PWK $17.95

Hypnotize Yourself Out of Pain Now!, Item HYOP $14.95

The Depression Workbook, 2nd edition, Item DWR2 $19.95

Beating the Senior Blues, Item YCBS $17.95

Shared Confinement, Item SDCF $15.95

Hanbook of Clinical Psychopharmacology for Therpists, 3rd edition, Item HCP3 $55.95

Getting Your Life Back Together When You Have Schizophrenia Item GYLB $14.95

Do-It-Yourself Eye Movement Technique for Emotional Healing, Item DIYE $13.95

Stop the Anger Now, Item SAGN $17.95

The Self-Esteem Workbook, Item SEWB $18.95

The Habit Change Workbook, Item HBCW $19.95

The Memory Workbook, Item MMWB $18.95

The Anxiety & Phobia Workbook, 3rd edition, Item PHO3 $19.95

Beyond Anxiety & Phobia, Item BYAP $19.95

The Healing Sorrow Workbook, Item HSW $17.95

The Anger Control Workbook, Item ACWB $17.95

The Relaxation & Stress Reduction Workbook, 5th edition, Item RS5 $19.95

Call **toll free, 1-800-748-6273,** or log on to our online bookstore at **www.newharbinger.com** to order. Have your Visa or Mastercard number ready. Or send a check for the titles you want to New Harbinger Publications, Inc., 5674 Shattuck Ave., Oakland, CA 94609. Include $4.50 for the first book and 75¢ for each additional book, to cover shipping and handling. (California residents please include appropriate sales tax.) Allow two to five weeks for delivery.

Prices subject to change without notice.